This work was created by the Education Justice Project. Copyright 2025, The Board of Trustees of the University of Illinois. All rights reserved. This work is licensed under a CC-BY-NC-SA 4.0.

ISBN: 979-8-9874811-8-9

# About *Mapping Your Future*

*Mapping Your Future* was made by members of the Education Justice Project (EJP). EJP is part of the College of Education at the University of Illinois at Urbana-Champaign. Since 2008, EJP has taught college courses to people incarcerated at Danville Correctional Center in Central Illinois.

We created *Mapping Your Future* because we care about people like you who are being released from prison. The guide is made by a group of committed EJP members called the Reentry Guide Initiative (RGI).

*Mapping Your Future* originally started as an Illinois reentry guide. Because we receive guide requests from people all over the U.S., we decided to create a national edition.

☆ **Disclaimer:** We have listed a lot of programs, services, and businesses in this guide as resources for formerly incarcerated people and their families. We don't endorse any of these organizations. We also don't guarantee that these resources will be helpful (although we hope they are).

The world is changing all the time. That means we can't be sure everything in this guide is up to date. Each version includes the best information we could find from trusted sources.

## Request Our Guides!

Both *Mapping Your Future* and *A New Path* are free for incarcerated or detained people.

They are available in English and Spanish and can be ordered here:
- educationjustice.net
- (217) 300-5150
- reentry@educationjustice.net
- Education Justice Project, Reentry Guide Initiative

    Education Justice Project
    1001 S Wright St
    Champaign, IL 61820

## Paying for Guides

We work hard to provide free copies of our reentry guide to all incarcerated or formerly incarcerated individuals who request them. Each copy of *Mapping Your Future* costs $12 to print and send. If you or your organization are able to pay, please send a check to the address above, or donate online at educationjustice.net/donate .

Please help us give *Mapping Your Future* to every person who wants it. Thank you!

Facing deportation to another country after release? Please request *A New Path: A Guide to the Challenges and Opportunities after Deportation*, available in English and Spanish, also from the Education Justice Project.

## Acknowledgments

*Mapping Your Future, National Edition 2024* is made possible by a generous grant from the Ascendium foundation (www.ascendiumphilanthropy.org .)

*Mapping Your Future, National Edition 2024* was revised and written by the following people:
- Lee Ragsdale, RGI Director
- Joshua Schriftman, Research and Writing Coordinator
- Manpreet Gurtatta, Outreach and Distribution Coordinator
- Christy Cannon, Guide Production Coordinator

**Advisory Committee:** Josephine Horace, Pablo Mendoza, Chad Rand, Jay Villa, Milton Callahan, and Anthony Hayes

**RGI Members:** Lili Burciaga, MoDena Stinnette, Kendra Mills, Amber Scarborough, Leanne Knobloch, Xochitl Guerrero, Ira Shinn, Gillian Snyder, Natalia Fic, Elisabeth Pollock, Linda Larsen, Ishita Jadon, Marco Wilson, Araceli Pantoja, and Katia Rodriguez

**RGI Interns:** Sarah Coffman, Celia Beaty, Kara Johnson, Yasmen Pugh, Veronica Siewierski

**Designers:** Jack Johnson, Jamarri Nix, Ashley Jung, and Surface 51

**Translators:** Araceli Pantoja and Eduardo Villafaña

**Special thanks to:**
- Rebecca Ginsburg, EJP Director
- Jamie Hines, EJP Operations Director

We gratefully acknowledge the many additional RGI members who have contributed to past editions of Mapping Your Future: Linda Larsen, Nick Hopkins, Emmett Sanders, Liliane Windsor, Millie Wright, Chris Rivers, Maggie Shelledy, Elise Duwe, Lauren Rodriguez-Golstein, Anita Greenfield, Rea Zaimi, Hugh Bishop, Logan Middleton, Ellen Ritter, David Sharpe, Antonio Spraggs, Karolina Karlota, Enddy Almonord, Sarah Chitwood, and Marlena Johnson.

We would also like to thank EJP alumni and other systems-impacted individuals for contributing content and images: Brian N., Chris H., Darrell W., Earl W., Edmund B., Greg A., Heather B., Jobie T., Johnny P., Keke, Marlon C., Mike T., Shawn W., Tony C., Roberto B., Dennis M., Joseph B., Austin C., Tyrone M., Pablo M., Mike C., Ricky H., Joseph M., Keiahty J., Robert R., MoDena S., David T., Edmund B., Michael H., Nicole L., Heather C., Alaina H., Jaqueline F., Flor E., Angel P., Kenneth D., Cassandra O., Raylan G., Linda S., Mackenzie K., Danielle W., Megan S., James F., and Orlando M.

# Welcome Home!

We're glad you picked up *Mapping Your Future: A Guide to Successful Reentry, National Edition.* Whether you spent many years in prison or just a few, it can help you start your life on the outside. This guide gives you information about employment, housing, education, healthcare, and more. It has resources for people throughout the US.

If you are a service provider, family member, or friend of someone who is coming home, this book can help you too. We hope you will find the information and support you need as well.

*Mapping Your Future* **has four sections:**

- **Before You Leave** gives advice about getting ready for release.
- **Once You're Out** helps you set up your life once you're out.
- **Healing and Moving Forward** is about getting used to life after prison.
- **The Reentry Directory** contains useful resources.

Getting used to life on the outside is hard. In prison you were separated from your loved ones, and it was expensive to stay connected. Prison life changes you. You may face a lot of challenges because of your record. You may have trouble finding a job. People might treat you differently. Your parole may feel unfair. Sometimes you might feel like there are too many challenges in your path! How can you succeed?

Mapping Your Future will help you meet the challenges. Maybe it will even make you want to work for change. We believe in YOU and your ability to make a difference in the world. Don't stop believing in yourself.

In this book, you'll find helpful words from people like you who went through reentry. Many of them are alumni of the EJP college-in-prison program at Danville Correctional Center in Illinois. It was their idea to produce Mapping Your Future. They, and so many others, have successfully reentered the outside world. You can too.

If you have time, it is best to read the entire guide. You can also skip around to the parts that are most important to you. Are you borrowing this guide from a friend or a counselor? **Write to us to request your own copy to take home with you.**

Please keep in touch. We'd love to know how you're doing and how we can make Mapping Your Future better. Your comments can help those who follow in your footsteps.

Again, welcome home. We're glad you're back.

In solidarity,

   the Education Justice Project

# Table of Contents

Myths ................................................................................................................. 8

## 1. BEFORE YOU LEAVE

Prepare Mentally for Release ............................................................................. 10
- Connect with Family and Friends
- Prepare for Challenges
- Know Your Strengths

Gather Your Documents ..................................................................................... 13

Prepare for Your Job Search ............................................................................... 16

Find Housing ..................................................................................................... 18
- Transitional Housing

Health Before Release ........................................................................................ 19
- Enroll in Medicaid
- Get Your Health Records
- Get Your Exams
- Make a Birth Control and Sexual Health Plan
- Make a Medication Plan
- Plan for Doctor Visits After Release
- Healthcare Checklist

Preparing for Reunification ................................................................................ 22
- Staying Close to Loved Ones
- Preparing for Reunification
- Preparing to Reunite with Children

Parole ............................................................................................................... 26
- Preparing for Parole
- Parole After Release
- Parole Rules and Violations
- Registries

## 2. AFTER YOU GET OUT

Getting Your ID .................................................................................................. 30
- State ID or Driver's License

Resources to Meet Your Basic Needs ................................................................. 32
- Apply for Benefits

Housing After Release ....................................................................................... 35
- Transitional Housing
- Emergency Shelters
- Subsidized and Public Housing
- Private Housing
- Renting an Apartment
- Help With Rent
- Your Legal Rights
- Housing for People with Sex Offense Convictions

Employment ...................................................................................................... 40
- Employment Resources
- Make a Plan
- Job Planning Worksheet
- Popular Career Options
- Women and Employment
- Look for Jobs
- Your Legal Rights
- Unemployment Benefits

Mapping Your Future, National Edition

Education ..................................................................................................................57
- ABE, GED, and High School Equivalency Programs
- Vocational Training and Apprenticeships
- College
- Paying for Your Education
- Resources for College Students

Health ......................................................................................................................62
- Health Insurance
- Dental and Vision Care
- Doctor Visits
- Pharmacy
- COVID-19
- HIV/AIDS and Other Diseases

Trauma and Mental Health ..................................................................................68
- Trauma
- Bouncing Back
- Caring for Your Mental Health
- Attitudes About Mental Health
- Common Mental Health Difficulties

Substance Use .......................................................................................................76
- Where to Get Help
- Safer Drug Use
- Treatment Programs
- Finding a Peer Support Group
- The Road to Recovery
- New Cannabis Laws

Transportation .......................................................................................................83
- Transportation Options
- Buying a Car
- Driving Legally

Technology .............................................................................................................86
- Getting a Phone
- Technology Basics
- Using the Internet
- Email, Passwords, and Security
- Smartphone Apps
- Social Media
- Video Conferencing
- Digital Literacy Resources

Legal Matters ........................................................................................................92
- Getting Legal Help
- Child Custody
- Child Support
- Fees and Fines
- Expunging or Sealing Records
- Certificates of Rehabilitation
- Executive Clemency

Finances, Credit, and Taxes ...............................................................................96
- Banking Basics
- Using Bank Cards for Purchases
- Budgeting and Financial Resources
- Avoiding Scams
- Credit
- Filing Taxes

Voting ....................................................................................................................104

Veterans ...............................................................................................................106
- Transferring Benefits to Your Family
- Reinstating Benefits After Release
- Filing Disability Claims
- Health
- Housing
- Employment

LGBTQ+ People ...................................................................................................109

## 3. HEALING AND MOVING FORWARD

Beginning to Heal .................................................................................................................. 112
Building Healthy Relationships ............................................................................................ 114
- *Self-Advocacy*
- *Sharing (Self-Disclosure)*
- *Asking for Help and Setting Boundaries*
- *Parenting After Release*
- *Dealing with Difficult Emotions*
- *Institutionalization*
- *Domestic Violence*

Mindfulness ........................................................................................................................... 126
- *What Is Mindfulness?*
- *What Are the Benefits of Mindfulness?*
- *How Do I Meditate?*
- *Meditation Scripts*
- *Meditation Resources*
- *Meditation Groups*

Connecting with Your Community ........................................................................................ 132
- *Community Organizing and Advocacy*
- *Getting Involved in Your Community*
- *Serving Your Community*

## 4. DIRECTORY

National Resources ............................................................................................................... 135
State Resources .................................................................................................................... 140

## 5. FORMS

Social Security Card Request Form ..................................................................................... 160
Sample Resumes ................................................................................................................... 161
Veterans Beneficiary Appointment Form ............................................................................. 164

# Myths

What kind of information will you find in this guide? For one thing, it will show you how some common myths you might have heard aren't true. Here are a few:

### No one will hire you if you've been incarcerated.

**False.** You can find a job. Persistence and patience will be needed. Some states have "Ban the Box" laws that mean employers can't run background checks until after they have offered you the job. Learn more in the Employment chapter (see p. 40).

### You have to pay for all your own medicine after you leave prison.

**Not exactly.** It is true that you will have to pay for your medication, but some prisons will give you a small amount of medicine when you leave. See the Health Before Release chapter to find out more (on p. 19).

### You can't get financial aid for college if you have been incarcerated.

**False.** If you are on parole or probation, you can get most financial aid. For more information about education options and how to apply for financial aid, see the Education chapter (on p. 57).

### You can't get a bank account if you have been incarcerated.

**False.** You can open a bank account, though you will still have to meet their requirements. For more information about banking, see our Finances, Credit, and Taxes chapter (on p. 96).

### You can get Social Security benefits for your time in prison.

**False.** You cannot get Social Security benefits while you are in prison. But if you were getting Social Security before you went to prison you can start getting it again. See the Resources to Meet Basic Needs chapter (on p. 32).

### You can't receive VA benefits after being incarcerated.

**False.** If you are a veteran, you can have your benefits restarted 30 days before your release date. See the Veterans chapter and the tear-out Veterans Beneficiary Apportionment form on pages 106 and 164.

### Health insurance costs too much. It is easier to pay healthcare costs out of pocket.

**False.** Health insurance can be expensive, but there are good options. If you don't have insurance, you'll pay much more if you go to the emergency room. See our Health chapter (on p. 62).

# Part 1:
# Before You Leave

- Prepare Mentally for Release
- Gather Your Documents
- Prepare for Your Job Search
- Find Housing
- Health Before Release
- Preparing for Reunification
- Parole

# Prepare Mentally for Release

It's never too early to get ready to leave prison. Even if you have a very long sentence, keep your eye on life after release. Find ways to learn and grow while you are there.

- Take Adult Basic Education (ABE) classes or get your GED.
- Take college classes or vocational classes.
- Meditate, play an instrument, draw, join a choir or read a book.
- Start going to religious services.
- Attend substance use programs or anger management classes.
- Get involved in volunteer activities.

These activities can help you meet other people who can support you. They will help you move beyond thinking of yourself as just a prisoner who has nothing to offer. In fact, we think you have a lot to offer!

You can still make a difference in prison. Education Justice Project (EJP) students at Danville Correctional Center in Central Illinois created a program to teach English to others behind bars. They run anti-violence discussion groups in the prison. Many incarcerated people donate to local charities or tutor people on the inside. What can you do?

Reentry is very hard. You will need to accept that things may not be perfect or easy. Forgive yourself if you make mistakes. You will probably have some awkward talks with people on the outside. Let yourself laugh them off. People in the outside world have awkward experiences all the time! You may think everyone will know you've just gotten out of prison, but they probably will not.

Patience is important on the outside. Everything may not go the way you want it to. It may be hard to find a job or reunite with loved ones. Sometimes you will feel confused by how much things have changed since you went away. Go slow. Breathe. It is normal to feel stressed sometimes, but you don't want it to get out of hand.

How will you relax once you're out in the world? Life on the outside can feel very rushed. EJP graduates said visiting Lake Michigan, taking long walks, biking, and gardening have helped. How will you include activities like this in your life?

You might learn to practice mindfulness. On the outside, mindfulness courses are offered through some hospitals, social services, and a few churches. The chapter on mindfulness (see p. 126) has a lot of advice on getting started and even has a few guided meditations.

# Connect with Family and Friends

People often isolate themselves during tough times. But it can help to stay connected to positive friends and family members. Think about the people you know. Who are the people you're counting on to be there for you?

Contact family members and friends. Be honest about what you need from them, whether it's housing, help with money, or just support and love. Find out what they expect from you.

Use this "Getting Ready to Get Out" checklist to help you plan your release. You can use this checklist to find out what areas would be useful for you to start working on now.

# Prepare for Challenges

Before leaving prison, work on practicing patience, both with others and yourself.

What skills do you use to manage stress?

When things go wrong, or when you're disappointed, what can you do to keep yourself on track and focused?

# Know Your Strengths

What have you done in the past to successfully adjust to major life changes?

What skills, habits, or traits helped you to stay motivated, build positive relationships, and maintain self-respect?

> *Best thing that can reduce anxiety is to have a plan. You don't have to be rigid with that plan because you're going to get out and realize that the world isn't what you expected it to be.*
>
> **—Joe Joe**

| Issues you may face upon release | Got this covered | Need to address |
|---|---|---|
| Substance use | | |
| Making ends meet | | |
| Family issues | | |
| Housing | | |
| Medical | | |
| Mental health | | |
| Transportation | | |
| Child care | | |
| Telephone | | |
| Pending legal issues | | |
| Child support status | | |

# Gather Your Documents

As your release date gets closer, you should start the process of getting your **birth certificate, Social Security card, and state ID.** You will need them as you seek employment, housing, health care, and more. It is harder to get them on the outside. Try to begin this process at least **one year** before you are released.

There may be counselors or departments at your facility that can help you get your documents. You will need to reach out to them and ask.

*Find out what programs, classes, or resources are available to prepare for release. Sometimes that stuff is hidden. Make inquiries into what necessary steps you must take to secure documents that would assist you with housing, identification, mental health services, as well as food and clothes shelters in your area.*

**—Kilroy**

*Take responsibility and look for as much information as you can. Go talk to the law clerks, everybody that you can to get information.*

**—Anonymous**

### STEP 1
## Verification of Incarceration

To get started, ask for a document that verifies that you are incarcerated (sometimes called a Verification of Incarceration). You may need this to get your other documents. It's also a good idea to gather any transcripts or certificates from classes you've taken in prison. You can use those documents to get your birth certificate, Social Security card, and state ID.

## STEP 2
# Birth Certificate

Next, you will need a certified copy of your birth certificate. This means a birth certificate that has a state seal and is signed and dated by the county registrar.

To get a birth certificate, you will need to mail a form to the county clerk in the county where you were born. Ask your prison library or a counselor for the form and for the address of the county clerk. You can also go to usa.gov to find a list of county clerk offices in your state. Fill out the form and mail it to the address on the form.

In some states, your counselor or clinical services department may take care of this for you. You may need your verification of incarceration, proof of address, and a fee.

When you get your birth certificate, put it in your master file to keep it safe.

If you cannot get your birth certificate before you get out, you can request it at a county clerk's office after you are released. Call them before you visit to get instructions.

## STEP 3
# Social Security Card

All US citizens and permanent residents have a Social Security number (SSN). This number is used by the government to keep track of your taxes and Social Security benefits. You will need your Social Security card when you get a job or open a bank account. If you have lost your card, you can apply for a new one. There is no fee for requesting your Social Security card.

To get your Social Security card while you are in prison, use the form in the back of this guide to request a card by mail. You can also request a form from your prison library or your counselor. To get a Social Security card you will need:

- A document that verifies you are incarcerated (Step 1)
- Your birth certificate (Step 2)
- A second document with your name and current address, such as HIV test results, a GED certificate, a transcript from a prison education program, or medical records

Make sure your Social Security card stays in a safe place, such as your master file, until you are released. Be aware that sharing it with another person could put you at risk for fraud.

*[Once I was out,] I needed a second form of identification to get my Social Security card. If you are in this sort of dilemma, you can retrieve a copy of your medical record as a second ID. If you do not have your medical record, you can go to a free clinic, take an H.I.V. test, and request a copy of the record; you can use this document along with your birth certificate to get your Social Security card.*

**—Antonio**

STEP 4
# State ID

To get a state ID, you will likely need:

- A document that verifies you are incarcerated (Step 1)
- Your birth certificate (Step 2)
- Your Social Security card (Step 3)
- A fee

However, since the procedure for getting an ID varies by state, it's best to ask your counselor or your prison library how to get yours. If you can't get your ID before you leave, ask your facility if they can offer you an ID verification form or temporary ID card. You will still need to get your state ID once you are out.

**If you are under an alias:** If you are locked up under an alias, it is really important that you start gathering your documents early. First, write to the county where you are convicted or the state's attorney office. Ask them to change the charging document to reflect your real name. The court probably will not change all of the court documents to fix this problem. You may need to talk to a lawyer to see if there are any legal steps you can take.

# Pulling Together Your Documents

Use this table to keep track of some of the documents and forms of ID you may need after you are released. Start gathering them now.

| Item | Taken care of | Need to tackle | Not applicable |
|---|---|---|---|
| Social Security card | | | |
| Birth certificate | | | |
| Temporary ID | | | |
| State ID or driver's license | | | |
| Marriage license | | | |
| Divorce decree | | | |
| Passport or green card | | | |
| Military discharge | | | |

 You can get marriage licenses and divorce decrees at the county clerk's office in which you were married or divorced.

Mapping Your Future, National Edition

# Prepare for Your Job Search

If you are getting ready to leave prison, you're probably thinking about getting a job. This is an area where you are likely to hit many roadblocks and challenges. The good news is that there are employers who are willing to give you a chance. There are ways you can prepare while still in prison to find a good job. Be hopeful. Many people have found good jobs after incarceration. If you're prepared, persistent, and have the right attitude, you can find one too.

### STEP 1
## Build Experience

In the facility where you're locked up, can you earn certificates, learn new skills, or work? Any experience like this can help you find a job on the outside. They can also make you more confident and help you build skills you didn't know you had.

School is another good way to get ready for work on the outside. Enroll in school programs, from Adult Basic Education to college programs. School records can also show employers you are intelligent and dedicated. Try other things too. Arts, parenting classes, and other programs will give you new skills and confidence.

### STEP 2
## Write Your Resume

Another important thing you can do while you're in prison is to write your resume. A resume is a summary of your skills, education, and work experience. You will need a resume to search and apply for jobs. Even if you don't have a computer or typewriter, write your resume out while you are still incarcerated. You can type it out after your release. Your resume should have several parts:

1. **Name, address, and contact information.** If you are not sure of your address yet, ask a friend or family member if you can use theirs.
2. **Education.** Your resume should have a list of schools you've attended. Add any education you had in prison, especially if you earned any degrees or certificates.
3. **Work experience.** List your jobs, including volunteer work. Include where, when, and for how long you held each job.
4. **Other professional skills.** This includes certifications, technical skills, and languages you speak other than English.
5. **Awards** (optional). If you've ever received an award for your work, like employee of the month, or a scholarship, list them at the end of your resume.

Are you worried what people will think when they see school or work you did in prison? You do not have to put those on your resume if it worries you. The sample resumes in the back of the book (see p. 161) can show you how other formerly incarcerated people have created their resumes.

For information about how to find and apply for jobs once you are released, see the Employment chapter (on p. 40).

*Be ready to pivot. Be patient with yourself. You're eager to get out, eager to do all of those things. Be realistic with yourself, what you can really do, what is within your control. You're going to be facing a lot of things.*

**—Roberto**

*If you sat at a table playing cards for ten years and now you want to come out and you want to go out and get yourself a job that's paying $18-20 an hour — well, be realistic. You're not gonna do it. You're not going to have that job because you didn't do anything to prepare. What are you going to put on your resume, that you played cards for ten years?*

**—Anonymous**

# Find Housing

## Transitional Housing

If you are not able to live with family members or friends upon release, you may live in a halfway house or transitional house. Some transitional houses allow people to stay six months, others up to two years. Some are free. Others might ask you to pay some of your income if you are working.

Many transitional housing programs provide support services, such as employment help, case management, life skills training, and medical referrals. Some programs help people recover from drug and alcohol addictions (often called "recovery homes"). Transitional houses usually have strict rules. They might have a curfew, or you might have to have a job or attend religious services.

> **Note:** The terms "halfway house" and "transitional housing" often mean the same thing.

## How to Find Housing

In many states, counselors will call you a few days before your release to place you in a halfway house. A lot of people need these spots. It's hard for them to know ahead of time what will be available. This can create a lot of stress. It may be useful to bring a list of transitional housing/halfway houses to your counselor.

Here are a few national websites that can help:

- Transitionalhousing.org
- Homelessshelterdirectory.org
- Shelterlistings.org
- Soberhousedirectory.com

The resource directories at the end of this book (see p. 135) list other national resources and many state-specific reentry organizations that may be able to help you find housing.

## Finding the Right Fit

There are a lot of good and bad transitional housing out there. Here are a few questions you can ask your counselor or the people at the transitional house to see if it is a good fit for you:

- Whom do you welcome?
- How long can I stay?
- What is the cost?
- What programs and services are offered? What will I be doing when I live there?
- Do you provide mental health or substance use treatment?
- What restrictions will I have while I am there? What freedoms will I have?
- Is this a faith-based program? Will I be required to attend services?

Most transitional houses do not let in people who have been convicted of sex offenses (see Housing for People with Sex Offense Convictions on p. 39), and some do not let in people who have been convicted of violent offenses.

# Health Before Release

Planning for health care before you leave prison saves money and helps you avoid problems. There are a few steps you can take before you are released.

 ## Enroll in Medicaid

Depending on your state and facility, you may be able to apply for Medicaid before you leave. Ask your counselor to help you get started. If you have a loved one with internet access, they may be able to help you apply at healthcare.gov . Once you submit your application, it takes 30 days to get insurance, so get started early! This is especially important if you have a health problem that requires treatment.

 ## Get Your Health Records

Ask your counselor about how to get your health records. You may need to fill out a form. We recommend that you start this process a few months before your release.

 ## Get Your Exams

Request a dental exam, an eye exam, and a physical exam before you leave prison. Start early (a year before release) in case they find something you will need to address.

 ## Make a Birth Control and Sexual Health Plan

If you plan to be sexually active after release, discuss birth control and safe sex during your physical exam. This may help you avoid an unwanted pregnancy or STD. Consider your options carefully. Some forms of birth control, like condoms, are easy to get and are fairly cheap. However, they need to be used every time you have sex and may not be as effective as other options. Other kinds of birth control require a prescription from a doctor or a medical procedure.

Women, during their physical exam, may be able to request longer-term birth control options, like pills, patches, or intrauterine devices (IUDs). Implants or IUDs can protect you for several years from unwanted pregnancy. Women should also request a gynecological exam with a PAP smear and ask for a mammogram if over age 40.

Mapping Your Future, National Edition

Unfortunately, some doctors working in prisons have pressured women to have hysterectomies (sterilization) and men to have vasectomies. While vasectomies are reversible through a second surgical procedure, hysterectomies will prevent you from ever conceiving. No doctor should pressure you into a permanent or long-term birth control or sterilization procedure. Take time to ask questions and decide what is best for you. **If you are feeling pressured, remember: it's your right to say no.**

# Make a Medication Plan

Many prisons offer people a 30-to-90-day supply of medication upon release. Generally, you will pick up your medications the day before you are released, but you may want to request these medications ahead of time, just to be safe. The doctor will usually give you a prescription so you can get more. Make a plan to get more medication after you leave. Set up an appointment with a doctor on the outside so that you don't run out. This can help you avoid going to the ER to get medications filled, which can be costly.

# Plan for Doctor Visits After Release

Before you are released, ask for a list of low-cost community clinics or healthcare providers that accept Medicaid. If you have a serious mental or physical health issue, or will need regular prescription refills, be proactive and set up appointments ahead of time. A counselor or family member may be able to set up the appointment for you.

You may have been in a drug or alcohol treatment program while in prison. Continue treatment after release to make sure you don't relapse. Ask your doctor, clinical services, or a family member to help you find a treatment center. Try to schedule the appointment for a few days after your release. The directory (see p. 135) includes a list of many low-cost health clinics and substance-use treatment centers.

**A warning:** The first few hours, days, and weeks after release are often the hardest. People are at greater risk for suicide. Many return to old habits, like drug or alcohol use. People are at greater risk for overdose because their bodies aren't used to drugs anymore. It is important to be proactive and schedule appointments with healthcare providers ahead of time. You may not need them, but you'll have a plan just in case.

For more information, see the Health chapter (on p. 62), the Trauma and Mental Health chapter (on p. 68), and the Substance Use chapter (on p. 76).

# Healthcare Checklist

| Action | Taken care of | Need to tackle | Where to get help |
|---|---|---|---|
| Enroll in Medicaid | | | |
| Get health records | | | |
| Physical exam | | | |
| Eye exam | | | |
| Dental exam | | | |
| Contraception plan | | | |
| Medication plan | | | |
| Enroll in SNAP | | | |
| Set up doctor visits after release | | | |
| Set up mental health treatment after release | | | |
| Set up substance use treatment after release | | | |
| Find a support group | | | |

# Preparing for Reunification

This chapter covers the following topics:
- Staying Close to Loved Ones
- Preparing for Reunification
- Preparing to Reunite with Children

 ## Staying Close to Loved Ones

For many, the hardest part of being locked up is the strain it places on relationships. The separation is hard for both you and your loved ones. While you may feel love, concern, and care, there may also be feelings of guilt, loss, frustration, anger, and grief.

*If you have any emotions at all, you're going to have guilt about making your family suffer the pains that you're going through. Because you're not suffering alone. They suffer with you while you're in there.*

**—Tony C.**

Healthy relationships are open, honest, and deep. When possible, try to maintain regular, open lines of communication through letters and phone calls. Staying in touch with your loved ones will make reunion easier on everyone.

*The complexities of being in prison can startle any relationship. That's why understanding and communication is key. In reality no one wants to be a burden; however, everybody needs someone. The pressure of maintaining a healthy relationship is hard for two people in the free world. When I was doing time, I had to understand the sacrifices I needed to make to maintain a healthy relationship with the people that mattered the most to me. I had to remember what it was like to be free, and I had to educate my family and friends of what it was like to be incarcerated.*

**—Antonio**

*A lot of times, people get discouraged when family don't take their phone calls. They don't get a response, and they get discouraged. They think, "To hell with it, they don't want to hear from me." Even if they don't respond, you still have to try to cultivate those relationships. A lot of times people are super busy out here. It's not that they don't want to talk to you. Keep cultivating those relationships because they are what's going to help you when you get out.*

**—Anonymous**

*It's hard, but you have to make your kids understand that you don't want to be away from them…. You love them and you're going to do everything you can to make sure you're in their life.*

**—Tony C.**

During incarceration, some relationships may end, and all relationships will be challenged. Some find it so difficult that they distance themselves as a form of self-preservation. Be aware that this distance can be very hard to overcome upon release.

> *You spend so many years in there and so much time keeping people at an arm's distance. You never let anybody get close.... But when you come home, you've gotten so used to keeping people at a distance that you just continue to do it. It's hard to make new friends.*
>
> **—Tony C.**

> *You don't want to worry your family with those issues. You get on the phone, and you grind your teeth. Regardless of what you're feeling, you're going to tell them that everything is going to be OK. You get in this habit of keeping things bottled up, and you're dealing with some degree of loneliness and emptiness, because you're not sharing it with your family.*
>
> **—Roberto**

Explore other ways to maintain relationships. While it's painful to not be physically present in your loved ones' lives, there are other ways to be present. Talk, listen, and provide emotional and mental support when and however you can.

> *Try to find ways to make it easier for them to accept you being gone. Because if you just sit and tell them how horrible it is and you bark at them every time they come to visit you or you yell at them in letters or on the phone, then they're gonna get frustrated with dad and say, "Well hey, you're not even here, so what can you do?"*
>
> **—Tony C.**

Relationships aren't a one-way street. Family members can also do a lot to maintain relationships. They can help those who are incarcerated feel included. Share everyday things to help them feel connected.

> *I send him a little bit of money, enough to keep phone calls going, you know, and pictures and stuff and try to set up options for him so he knows he doesn't have to go back to the same stuff. Just let him know that there's help, there's better things in life. I try to talk to him about the good stuff, about working and going to church, when we're playing games with his little sister and stuff like that.*
>
> **—Heather B.**

# Preparing for Reunification

You might be scared, worried, or excited about reuniting with family and friends. You can prepare by reflecting on your relationships. Be honest about who is likely to be a positive, supportive influence in your life. You and your loved ones can also set realistic expectations. You are all in transition. A period of adjustment will be necessary.

It is hard to be left at home and hard to come home, even if you were only away for a few months. For loved ones, having the person come home can take some getting used to as well.

You might begin by letting your loved ones know what you are hoping for and what you will need from them during your reentry. This could include both emotional and financial support. Never be afraid to ask for patience.

Listen to the needs and concerns of your loved ones, too. Reuniting will be easier if you can talk ahead of time and learn to compromise.

*The key thing is honesty. [If] you come out being honest with yourself and with [your loved ones], you can't go wrong, because you're not feeding them a fairy tale. You're giving them you.*

**—Keke**

*Keep in mind that you are entering somebody else's space. You must be mindful of the relationships around you.*

**—Pablo**

If you were locked up for a long time, you'll need to relearn who you are and who your loved ones are. Children who were young when you left may be teenagers or even grown up with children of their own. You may have different ideas of what the new relationship should look like.

*Don't come in like they're supposed to know you or even respect you a little bit, because you've been gone. You gotta gain that respect and that trust back when you've been gone so long.*

**—Keke**

*Recognize that we haven't been part of that house for years, so I can't come in and put down my dominance, something we're used to doing when we're in the cell. We're used to carving up space and making it our own.*

**—Joe Joe**

Acknowledge the ways you have changed. You and your loved ones have both grown. Allow for this growth. Be open to the person before you and who they are now.

*First you gotta get yourself together, mentally. Because you might think you know them because they're part of you, but you really don't know them and what they've been through. You know what they tell you. Same thing with you.*

**—Keke**

*Never expect anyone to evolve at your pace. When you are dealing with people you haven't lived with in a while, you have to be analytical, you have to examine the structure of your own character. And the character of those you live with. Once you are fully in tune with the compound presence of your household, you should become as flexible as a bamboo stick, but it won't be easy. So, get an evaluation and accept some help from those who can help you with your transition.*

**—Antonio**

*Oftentimes when people are anticipating going home, they have ideals and expectations on how their reunification with family will be. There's the dream and there's the reality. It's good to have these great expectations, but don't set yourself up for disappointment if people don't live up to the expectations you have of them. People have lived experience that might color the way they interact.*

**—Joe Joe**

# Preparing to Reunite with Children

You may have young children you are looking forward to being with. You may be excited to see your kids again, or you might be nervous and stressed. You might feel both of these things. It's ok to have mixed feelings. There's no right way to feel.

There are things you can do to parent from prison and prepare yourself for regaining custody of your kids, if that's your goal. Show your commitment to your children. This will make it easier to get them back when you are out. Here are some ideas:

| **Before your release** | **After your release** |
|---|---|
| Stay in touch with your kids through regular phone calls and letters. Record the dates and times so that you have evidence of your involvement. | Prioritize getting safe and stable housing. |
| Attend all hearings about your child. It's your right! | Follow all parole rules and requirements. |
| Take parenting classes if offered. | Visit your kids as often as you can. Record details about the visits. |
| Take job training as well as academic and technical classes. | Continue to attend parenting, job training, or other classes. This shows your commitment to providing a stable home for your child. |

If you've been separated from your children, you may be eager to reunite with them as soon as you can. But don't rush things. First you need to have a stable job, safe housing, and sobriety. Getting your kids back too soon can cause more harm than good if you are unable to provide a healthy and safe environment for them.

If your parental rights have been terminated, you will need the court's permission to get your children back. To find legal aid in your area, search for the name of your city and terms like "child custody" or "legal aid." "Pro bono" legal aid is offered for free.

Even if you don't get your kids back as soon as you would like, you can still make changes and be involved in decisions about them. If getting your kids back is what's right for your family, don't give up, even if there are roadblocks!

# Parole

When you are released from prison, you will probably be on some form of parole or probation. This means you will be supervised by the Department of Corrections for your state until your parole period is over.

While on parole, you'll have to follow some rules. It is frustrating to know that even though you are getting out of prison, you will not be completely free. Hang in there. Parole is difficult, but many people have gotten through it. You can, too.

This chapter covers:
- Preparing for Parole
- Parole After Release
- Parole Rules and Violations
- Registries

# Preparing for Parole

The parole process varies by state but usually begins around six months before your release date.

### STEP 1
### Educate yourself about the conditions of your release.

This may mean communicating with a parole board that will make plans for your parole conditions. For example, you may have to go to an anger management class, or you may be placed on electronic monitoring for a while.

### STEP 2
### Find a place to live.

In your parole plans, you will likely have to submit the address where you plan to live, which will need to be approved. A parole officer may have to visit the home and decide if it is OK for you to stay there, especially if you will be placed on electronic monitoring.

### STEP 3
### Talk to the people you will be living with.

Many of the parole rules you'll follow will affect the people you will be living with. Talk to them early and clearly. Let them know what your parole rules will mean for them. They can contact your state's department of corrections with their questions.

### STEP 4
## Complete paperwork.

The people you will be living with may have to complete a document that allows them to host you in their home. It may come in the mail, or the parole officer may bring it when they visit the home.

**Transferring parole to another state.** If you plan to live in another state, talk to your counselor about transferring your parole. They can let you know what to do to transfer.

# Parole After Release

Your parole rules will probably require that you contact your parole officer right away, often within 24 hours of your reentry. Before you leave, make sure you have your parole officer's name and phone number. It is your job to get in touch with your parole officer. If you cannot reach your parole officer or do not know who they are, contact a nearby parole office for help.

When you call your parole officer, they may set up a visit with you in the next few days. Do not leave your home until your parole officer visits. This will usually happen within three days.

## Electronic Monitoring

Many people are placed on electronic monitoring. If you have been placed on electronic monitoring, you will have to follow some extra rules.

You will likely get instructions before you are released. You may need to go straight home and check in with your parole officer. Usually, a technician will then come to your home to set up the electronic monitor. The monitor may have an anklet and a box that plugs in the wall. Make sure the monitor stays plugged in. Once the monitor is set up, you and your parole officer will decide what times you will be allowed to leave your home.

You will be required to check in regularly with your parole officer. Remember, it's very important you answer the phone when the parole agency calls. Not answering could get you in trouble.

Electronic monitoring can be hard for everyone in your house. Until you find a job, you will be home most of the time, which can cause stress. If you need rides during your movement times, you will need to work that out. Talk clearly with the people you will live with. Let them know what you need from them, what they need from you, and how you will address problems.

# Parole Rules and Violations

Parole officers have the final say for parole rules. These rules are written in a legal document. Make sure you understand all of the rules and instructions before you sign. Ask questions! Some of the most common rules include:

- Do not commit any criminal acts.
- Report to your parole officer on a regular basis.
- Do not possess firearms.
- Allow the parole officer to inspect and search you and your residence.
- Refrain from using drugs.
- Do not leave the state.

Keep your documents in a safe place so you can get to them easily. Hold on to documents that explain the conditions of your probation or parole, your registration documents, and any receipts you collect in the process.

If you break the rules of parole, you may be sent back to prison. Sadly, this happens a lot. Follow the rules of your parole very carefully so you can stay on the outside. If something happens that makes it look like you broke your parole, call your parole officer right away to explain what happened. If you haven't broken any rules, your parole office can ask that you not be charged.

If you are charged with breaking parole, you may be able to appeal. You may be assigned a lawyer. The lawyer can show evidence and bring witnesses to help you make your case.

# Registries

Your state may require you to register after release, depending on your conviction. Many states have sex offense registries. There may be other registries, such as those for violent offenses or arson. These registries are online databases that anyone can see. They have photos and information, such as your name, address, birthday, place of work, crime conviction history, and the gender and age of the person you were convicted of harming.

If you have to register, you will likely face many challenges. People will make hurtful comments. It will be very hard to find housing and a job. Focus on your self worth. You are more than your conviction. We believe in you.

Before you are released, ask your counselor if you need to register. You can also ask someone you trust to contact the authority that maintains the registries. Make sure you know and understand the rules. It's easy to make a mistake and go back to jail. You may be charged with "failure to register" because you missed a deadline or didn't know you had to register more than once.

**Where will I register?** Typically, you will register at your local police or sheriff's department. This is something you will likely need to do right away when you get to your host site.

**How often will I need to register?** It depends. You may have to register every 90 days or once a year. Keep a calendar of all your registration deadlines. Call ahead and make appointments if you can.

**What should I bring when I register?** It varies by state. You will likely need proof of address (for example, a rental agreement, a bill for your rent or a utility bill, or another official document showing your address) and your state ID. They will take a photo of you and post it on the registry website. They may also take fingerprints or a DNA swab. You will have to sign registration documents. Be sure you understand what you are signing.

**How long will I have to register?** It depends on your conviction and the state you live in. You may be required to register every year for a few years after release. For more serious convictions, you may have to register for the rest of your life.

**Do I have to register every time I move?** Yes—though if you move out of state, check to find out their requirements. Some states do not have registries. Generally, you have a few days to let law enforcement know that you have moved. You may also have to re-register if you change jobs or if you change your email address or online identifiers (your names on social media, for example).

**Will I have to pay to register?** Check with your state. Illinois requires a fee of $100 or 100 hours of community service per year, and failure to pay is a felony.

**What other restrictions may I face?** Common restrictions, especially for those convicted of child sex offenses, include not being allowed to go in school buildings or on school grounds, or live near a school, playground, or childcare facility. You may not be allowed in parks or public park buildings. You may not be able to use social media, like Facebook or Instagram.

**Where can I get help?** You don't have to figure it out alone. There may be organizations in your state that can support you. The Sex Law and Policy Center publishes a reentry guide called Registering with Dignity. Check it out here: ncsecondchance.org/wp-content/uploads/2018/01/18Dec17RWDFinalwithCover_Corr.pdf .

☆ It is against the law to harass or threaten people on the sex offense registry or their families. If this is happening to you, call the police or your probation or parole officer.

# Part 2: After You Get Out

- Getting Your ID
- Resources to Meet Your Basic Needs
- Housing After Release
- Employment
- Education
- Health
- Trauma and Mental Health
- Substance Use
- Transportation
- Technology
- Legal Matters
- Finances, Credit, and Taxes
- Voting
- Veterans
- LGBTQ+ People

# Getting Your ID

Congratulations, you're out! If you weren't able to get an ID while you were incarcerated, this will be your first priority. Hopefully, you already have your birth certificate and Social Security card. If not, here's how you can get them:

- Call or go to the county clerk's office in the county where you were born. They can help you get your birth certificate.
- Go to a Social Security Administration Office to get your Social Security card. Call before you go to set up an appointment and find out what you need to bring.

☆ You can get marriage licenses and divorce decrees at the county clerk's office in which you were married or divorced.

 ## State ID or Driver's License

Once you have your birth certificate and Social Security card, you can get a state ID or driver's license. These are the most common forms of ID. To get either a state ID or a driver's license, you'll need to visit the Department of Motor Vehicles (DMV), sometimes called Driver Services, in your state.

Do you plan to get a driver's license? Read your state's Rules of the Road booklet first. You can pick up a copy of this booklet at any public library or download it from your state's DMV. If you've been incarcerated for a long time, we recommend getting a learner's permit. A learner's permit lets you practice driving until you feel comfortable taking the driver's test. To get a permit, you will need to pass a written test and a vision test. Once you get the permit, you can drive with another driver who has a license.

Visiting Driver Services can take a long time, so be sure to bring everything you need:
- An original document with your written signature (credit card, court order, or Social Security card)
- An original document with your date of birth (birth certificate, passport, high school transcript, or college transcript from classes you took in prison)
- An original document with your Social Security number (Social Security card, driver's license record, or military service record)
- Proof of address (bank statement, credit report, utility bills, medical record, or HIV test)
- Payment

**(By "original," we mean the actual document you received, not a copy of that document).**

*It took me seven months to get my Social Security card and ID; this time would have been cut in half if I would have been given the information shared here.*

**—Antonio**

## Suspensions

Is your license suspended? A license can get suspended for many reasons:

- Not paying traffic tickets, parking tickets, or tolls
- Being convicted of driving while drunk or using drugs (called Driving Under the Influence, or a DUI)
- Not making child support payments

If your license was suspended, you can get it back after the suspension period is over.

## Revocations

"Revoked" means your driver's license has been taken away. Driver's licenses are often revoked for serious DUIs. For example, if someone was injured because the driver was drunk or using drugs. If your license is revoked, you may be able to get a new one. But you will have to wait for some time.

If your license was revoked because someone was killed while you were driving, you may not be able to get a new one. But you should still check to be sure.

☆ If you choose to drive without a license, you may face more serious penalties (more time without a license, jail time, or losing your car).

## Getting Your License Back

How do you get your license back if it was suspended? First, contact your state's DMV or Driver Services. Ask them how long before you can apply for a new license. You should be able to find more information on this process at your state's DMV website, including hearing information.

*If you go with the frame of mind that you are going to spend a hell of a lot of time in that place[DMV], it helps. Go with the right frame of mind, otherwise you're going to be miserable.*

—**Anonymous**

## Signing up for the Selective Service

Did you know you may have to sign up for "the draft"? The draft is called the Selective Service. It is a program that lets the US military call men to serve. You need to register for Selective Service if you are:

- Male
- Between 18-25
- Are a US citizen or resident

Registering with the Selective Service does not mean you are in the military. It means you may be called to serve in the military if there is a crisis.

If you need to register for the Selective Service and you don't, you could be fined or go to jail. This could also disqualify you for government jobs or government training. You can register online at sss.gov/register . You can also pick up a registration form at any post office.

You don't have to register if you were incarcerated the entire time you were 18 to 25. You will need to request a status-information letter at www.sss.gov/verify/sil .

What if you weren't incarcerated but you still didn't register? You can also request a status-information letter. The letter should say that you did not "knowingly or willfully" fail to register for Selective Service. You could mention if you were incarcerated shortly after your 18th birthday, left school early, or anything else that might have made it hard to register.

*Make appointments for anything and everything. Don't wait until you have all the requirements in your hand. Just make the appointment. You can always reschedule if you need to.*

—**Roberto**

# Resources to Meet Your Basic Needs

Leaving prison is exciting but not always easy. Many people have trouble finding a place to live or buying food after they leave prison. Other people struggle with drug or alcohol use or mental health issues. Be patient with yourself. Take your time as you figure things out. There are places you can go for help.

This chapter has two main sections:
- How to apply for government benefits to meet your basic needs
- Other places to go to meet your basic needs

 # Apply for Benefits

Did you know the government can help you with some basic needs? One of the first things you should do after release is apply for government assistance programs. If you need help, go to a Department of Human Services (DHS) office. You can also visit a hospital, non-profit organization, church, or other service provider and ask for help applying for benefits.

To get these benefits, you'll have to meet certain qualifications. For some programs, you have to be a certain age. For most, you must meet income requirements (not make a lot of money).

Many benefit programs are offered by states. You can find more information on the following programs by searching for the name of the program and your state.

- **Supplemental Nutrition Assistance Program (SNAP)** used to be called "food stamps." Each month, money is put onto a special debit card called a LINK card. You can use the card to buy food from most grocery stores.
- **Medicaid** is for people who make little or no money. It helps people pay for medicine, hospital visits, doctor appointments, and more.
- **Temporary Assistance for Needy Families (TANF)** provides money for families who need it.
- **Aid to the Aged Blind and Disabled Cash Assistance (AABD)** provides money for people who have disabilities or who are blind.
- **Medicare Savings Program (MSP)** helps pay for the costs of Medicare for older people and people with disabilities. (See below for an explanation of Medicare).

When you sign up for benefits, ask if there are other services, too, like programs to help with rent and utilities, including internet or child care.

## Social Security Programs

The Social Security Administration has other benefit programs that you may be able to use now that you are out of prison, including the following:

- **Medicare** provides health insurance to people 65 or older and people with a disability. See www.ssa.gov/benefits/medicare/ .
- **Supplemental Security Income (SSI)** helps people 65 or older and adults and children who have a disability. It gives people money every month to help with things like food, clothing, and housing. See www.ssa.gov/benefits/ssi/ .
- **Social Security Disability Insurance (SSDI)** gives money to adults with disabilities and some of their family members. To use this program, you need to have worked for many years.
- **Social Security Retirement Benefits** are for people 62 or older. To get this money, you need to have worked before you went to prison.

**Note:** Almost all disability applications are rejected at first. If you don't qualify, don't give up. Keep trying.

Learn more and apply at ssa.gov , or call (800) 722-1213 for help. Get in-person help by making an appointment with your local Social Security office. Go to www.ssa.gov/locator .

## Benefits Checklist

| Program | Description | Do I qualify? | Have I applied? |
|---|---|---|---|
| SNAP | Money for food, LINK card | | |
| Medicaid | Healthcare help | | |
| TANF | Money for families in need | | |
| AABD | Money for those who are blind/disabled | | |
| Lifeline | Help with phone and internet payment | | |
| LIHEAP | Provides help with utility bills | | |
| Medicare | Health insurance for seniors, people with disabilities | | |
| SSI | Monthly payments for those with disabilities | | |
| SSDI | Monthly payments for those with disabilities | | |
| Social Security Retirement Benefits | Monthly payments for those who are retired | | |

Mapping Your Future, National Edition

# Places to Go For Help

| I need help with... | Where to get help | How to get help |
|---|---|---|
| Food | Food pantries, soup kitchens | Find one at www.feedingamerica.org/find-your-local-foodbank . |
| Health and dental care | Free or low-cost community health and dental clinics that don't require insurance<br><br>Go to an emergency room if you have an emergency. | Find a clinic at nafcclinics.org/find-clinic .<br><br>Call 911 if you're having an emergency. |
| Substance use treatment | Support group, treatment programs | Call the SAMHSA National Helpline at (800) 662-4357.<br><br>For support groups, go to aa.org (Alcoholics Anonymous) or na.org (Narcotics Anonymous). |
| Housing | Emergency housing, transitional housing | Go to www.hud.gov/findshelter . |
| Mental health (emergency) | The Suicide and Crisis Lifeline, hospital emergency rooms | Call 988 for the Suicide and Crisis Lifeline. Call 911 if you are having an emergency. |
| Mental health (non-emergency) | Mental health clinics that offer free or low-cost services | Go to findtreatment.samhsa.gov . |

*I came home after ten years, I went to a homeless shelter and three days later I had a job. A week and a half later, I had an apartment. My first paycheck, I got a cheap studio apartment. So you can do it. Don't let your feelings from being incarcerated judge who you are and what you can do. Because you can make it.*

**—Tony C.**

*The advice I would give is to be patient. Things in the outside world move very quickly and I think that you have to be aware and accepting that you don't have to catch up.*

**—Edmund B.**

# Housing After Release

Finding a place to live is one of the most important parts of the reentry process. It can also be one of the hardest parts. The challenge is to find housing that is accessible, low-cost, and stable. In some states, people on parole are not allowed to associate with other people with felony convictions. This may limit your choices, but other options are available.

This chapter covers the following topics:

- Transitional Housing (halfway houses)
- Emergency Shelters
- Subsidized and Public Housing
- Private Housing
- Renting an Apartment
- Help with Rent
- Your Legal Rights
- Housing for People with Sex Offense Convictions

## Transitional Housing

Many people who leave prison go to a halfway house or transitional house. Some transitional houses allow people to stay three months, others up to two years. If you are looking for transitional housing, please see the Find Housing chapter in Before You Leave (on p. 18).

## Emergency Shelters

If you find yourself without a place to stay, there are emergency shelters. Some shelters are for men only. Some are for women and children. Most do not allow people on the sex offense or violent offense registries. Many shelters offer food, laundry, and support services to help you find more permanent housing. Look for emergency housing in your state at www.shelterlistings.org .

## Subsidized and Public Housing

There are several different subsidized and public housing options. These options are supported by the government and have cheaper rents.

- **Public housing** is owned by the government. People who meet income requirements can live there. Contact your local Public Housing Authority (PHA) to find out about public housing in your area. Go to resources.hud.gov to find your PHA.
- **Section 8 housing** is a program where the government provides housing vouchers to help cover rent. You can live in a private apartment or house of your choice, and they will give you a voucher to help you pay for it. Section 8 housing is offered through your local Public Housing Authority (PHA). If you qualify, your PHA can provide a list of places where your vouchers can be used.

*Mapping Your Future, National Edition*

- **Project-based subsidized housing,** or affordable housing, is housing that is owned privately. The owners receive subsidies from the government to make their housing cheaper for low-income people and families. Your local PHA may also have a list of project-based subsidized housing.
- **Permanent supportive housing** may be available to you if you are a senior or veteran; if you have a disability, mental illness, or HIV/AIDS diagnosis; or if you have been homeless.. Permanent supportive housing includes support services, such as medical care and counseling. There is no limit to how long you can stay there. To find this type of housing, check with your state's Department of Human Services (DHS). Your state's local Housing and Urban Development (HUD) office may be able to provide information about this type of housing as well.

**Can I stay in public housing if I have a record?** This varies by state. In some places, people with criminal records cannot get public or subsidized housing. In states like Illinois, this is changing. The recently passed Public Housing Access Bill allows most people released from prison in Illinois to live in public housing upon reentry.

To find out if you are eligible for public housing, ask reentry organizations in your state, your parole officer, your state's Department of Human Services, or your regional HUD office or PHA. You can find these last two resources here: resources.hud.gov .

**How much does subsidized or public housing cost?** How much you pay for housing depends on how much money you earn. Many places will require you to pay 30 percent of your income to rent.

**How should I apply?** Public and subsidized housing programs often have long wait lists. You should apply as early as you can. Call your local PHA and ask for instructions, or apply online. To find your local housing authority visit www.hud.gov/program_offices/public_indian_housing/pha/contacts . Once you have applied, they will let you know when there is a place available. You can call and check to see where you are on the waiting list.

# Private Housing

Private housing can be easier to find than public housing because there is more of it. However, it also costs more. Private housing can be found online and in the classified section of newspapers. Some websites include:

- www.apartments.com
- www.zillow.com
- www.forrent.com
- www.craigslist.org
- www.trulia.com

You are likely to run into barriers because of your background. It may take a while to find a landlord who will rent to you. Large property management firms almost always conduct background checks, so you may have better luck with units in smaller complexes or in private homes. Sadly, we are not aware of any lists of landlords that rent to people who have been incarcerated.

Others who have come home from prison before you may be your best source of information. If you are part of a reentry program, use it as a resource. Use your network of friends and family. They may know of places where you can stay.

# Renting an Apartment

Once you've found an apartment, call the landlord and set up a time to view it. Arrive on time and dress nice. You want to give a good first impression.

At your visit, you may be asked to fill out an application and pay an application fee. The application will ask for information such as your employer, rent history, and current address. You may also be asked for references—people who can vouch for you, like employers or church leaders.

The application may also ask about your criminal history. Many landlords conduct background checks. You may worry that sharing your history will hurt your chance of getting the apartment. Even though this may be true, we suggest that you be up front if they ask. It may not disqualify you.

**Warning:** If anyone asks you for money before you have even seen the apartment, you are probably being scammed. Do not pay anything before you have seen the apartment.

Questions you might ask a landlord:

- What is the rent?
- How much is the security deposit?
- Is there an application fee?
- Are utilities included?
- When is the rent due?
- What is the parking like?
- Are tenants able to make changes (e.g., paint the walls)?
- Is there an additional cost for pets or other family members?
- Is there a background check? If so, who would be excluded from eligibility?
- What are the terms of the lease?
- When will the apartment be available?

If a landlord agrees to rent to you, you will sign a lease or a rental agreement.

- A **lease** is usually a year-long commitment, and you agree to pay a certain amount each month for the whole year.
- A **rental agreement** is typically month-by-month. After 30 days, both you or the landlord are free to back out or change the agreement.

Read the lease or rental agreement carefully before signing or paying any fees. It is legally binding. You won't be able to back out once you have signed. Keep a copy in a safe place.

**Security deposits.** Many landlords require one to two month's rent as well as a security deposit or move-in fee before you move in. The security deposit may be refunded to you when you move out, but the move-in fee will not. The security deposit or move-in fee shows that you are serious about renting the apartment. If you choose not to move into the apartment, the landlord keeps this money. Ask for a receipt for the security deposit and any other fees you pay.

When you move out, your security deposit will be used to cover any damages to the apartment that you caused. It's a good idea to take pictures of anything that is damaged when you move in so that you can show that you didn't cause it. Your landlord should not use your security deposit to pay for regular wear and tear of living in your apartment, but for items like a broken light fixture or carpet damage. You should receive a receipt for damages when you move out. Any leftover money from the security deposit should be mailed to you within 30 to 45 days.

**Breaking a lease.** If you need to move out before your lease ends, you can do so, but you will have to pay a fee. The amount that you pay should be listed in the lease, so read it carefully. You may have to keep paying rent until they find someone else to rent the apartment.

# Help with Rent

If you need help paying rent or utilities, there may be programs in your community that can help.

Check with your state's Department of Human Services (DHS) to see if they offer rental assistance programs. Here's a link to a list of rental assistance programs across the country: nlihc.org/rental-assistance . You can also get information on this type of resource and others by calling 211.

# Your Legal Rights

## Important Housing Laws

Below we've listed some of the housing laws to be aware of. If a landlord breaks one of these laws, you can file a complaint (see the Housing Discrimination section below). These laws apply if you are renting or buying a home, getting a mortgage, or seeking housing assistance.

### Federal Fair Housing Act

Landlords cannot discriminate based on race, color, national origin, religion, sex (including gender identity and sexual orientation), family status, or disability.

### HUD Fair Housing Act Guidelines

In 2016, HUD added guidelines for how the Fair Housing Act applies to people who have records:

- Arrest records and convictions can be used to deny people housing, but landlords cannot automatically refuse someone with a criminal record.
- The landlord must prove that they are refusing someone to protect their property or the safety of people living in their housing.
- In 2022, HUD released additional guidance for housing providers, encouraging them not to consider criminal history. If they do, they have to consider the individual's specific circumstances instead of excluding all individuals with convictions.

### State and City Specific Laws

Depending on where you live there may be additional laws that protect you from discrimination.

## Eviction

Are you worried about getting kicked out of your apartment? There are probably organizations in your community that can help. Do a search for the name of your community and key words like "eviction help" or "housing resources." HUD offers information about eviction at www.hud.gov/rent_relief , and you can find your local office in their online directory here: www.hud.gov/program_offices/field_policy_mgt/localoffices .

## Housing Discrimination

If you have been discriminated against, there are several ways you can file a complaint:

- You can file a complaint through HUD. Submit the complaint as soon as possible. Call them toll-free at (800) 669-9777 or (800) 877-8339, or email ComplaintsOffice05@hud.gov .
- You can file a complaint with the state where you live, possibly through its Department of Human Rights.
- You can file a complaint in the city where you live. You may be able to file a grievance at your city's Human Relations Commission or a similar regional agency.

## Legal Assistance

Here are a few resources that can help:

- Legal assistance for at-risk renters: localhousingsolutions.org/housing-policy-library/legal-assistance-for-at-risk-renters
- Eviction laws database: lsc.gov/initiatives/effect-state-local-laws-evictions/lsc-eviction-laws-database

# Housing for People with Sex Offense Convictions

Sadly, there are very few housing options that will accept people with sex offense convictions. We wish we had better news, but it is hard for people on registries to find housing.

Although it may be against your state's laws, sometimes people who are required to register have not been able to get out of prison because they could not find housing. They have stayed past the end of their prison sentence because they don't have a place to stay.

People who have a sex offense conviction and no permanent housing are asked to often check in with the registry. They may be asked to do this many times after they first register. They are also at greater risk of returning to prison—not because they reoffend, but because a lack of housing options leads them to violate the terms of their parole.

Still, there is hope. You may be able to live with family members, or there may be transitional houses in your state that serve people on the registries. You also may be able to find private housing.

**Help and advocacy:** We encourage you to reach out to organizations that might exist in your community for people with sex offense convictions, if you can find one. Here are a few resources to get you started:

- Information and tips on finding housing in different states: sexoffenderonestopresource.com/national-links
- "Registering With Dignity" handbook for people who are forced to register: ncsecondchance.org/resources/registering-with-dignity-a-practical-guide-for-reentry-and-life-on-the-registry

Mapping Your Future, National Edition

# Employment

You will hear a lot of discouraging talk about getting a job with a record. While it is hard, there are companies that are willing to hire people with records. Don't give up.

The good news is that there are lots of job openings right now. Many employers are having a hard time filling jobs. This doesn't mean it will be easy to find work, but you may have more options than you expect.

There is a lot involved with finding a job, so this is one of the longest chapters. It covers these topics:
- Employment Resources
- Make a Plan
- Job Planning Worksheet
- Popular Career Options
- Women and Employment
- Look for Jobs
- Your Legal Rights
- Unemployment Benefits

## Employment Resources

Finding a job and building a career is hard, especially with a criminal record. We strongly suggest that you find people or programs to help you. Here are a few places to start.
- **American Job Centers** help people search for jobs and find training. Go to careeronestop.org to find a location of an American Job Center near you. This website has many resources to help you with your job search. Call (877) 872-5627 for help.
- Your state may have a **Department of Employment Security** or other agency that helps people find jobs.
- **Reentry programs** and transitional housing organizations in your community may offer employment services.
- Your **parole or probation officer** may have ideas about jobs and training you could apply for.
- Go to guides.loc.gov/reentry-resources/employment for a list of helpful resources about employment for people who have been incarcerated.

## Make a Plan

For many people who leave prison, the goal is to get any job that pays, even if it isn't ideal. The job may not be something you want to do forever, but it can help you get back on your feet. It can lead to a better job in the future.

Even as you look for jobs to meet your basic needs, it's good to explore different careers. Find out what careers match your interests and skills. Look for careers that are in demand where you can earn good money. Learn about the training that you will need.

Take time to make a plan. Talk to a career counselor about your skills and interests and the kind of job you are looking for. You can use the worksheet on the following page to explore some of your career interests.

Here are a few of the many websites that can help you explore different careers:

- **careeronestop.org** . Explore careers, find training, check out their toolkit, search for jobs, and more.
- **mynextmove.org** . Explore careers and get information about what you can do to get a job.
- **myskillsmyfuture.org** . Find out how your skills, experience, and interests can lead to a new career.

We also recommend reading Take Charge of Your Future. This guide for formerly incarcerated people will help you take steps to get education and training for a career. It was developed by the US Department of Education. Request a FREE copy by calling (877) 433-7827 or emailing edpubs@edpubs.ed.gov . You can access it online here: www2.ed.gov/about/offices/list/ovae/pi/AdultEd/take-charge-your-future.pdf .

# Job Planning Worksheet

## Fill out this worksheet alone or with a mentor.

**What am I good at?** Knowing your strengths, gifts, and talents is an important first step.

_____

_____

_____

**What are my weaknesses?** What kinds of things are hard for you to do? What things don't come naturally to you?

_____

_____

_____

**What do I know how to do?** Take some time to think about your skills. This could include skills you learned on the job, in prison programs, or by caring for family members.

_____

_____

_____

## Check some of the things you like to do:

- ○ I like to work with people.
- ○ I like working with food.
- ○ I like working with animals.
- ○ I like routine.
- ○ I like using my hands.
- ○ I like working with computers.
- ○ I like solving problems.
- ○ I like building things.
- ○ I like being creative.
- ○ I like communicating with others.
- ○ I like making a difference.
- ○ I like helping people.
- ○ I like caring for people who are sick.
- ○ I like being part of a team.
- ○ I like being my own boss.
- ○ I like being a leader.
- ○ I like to work outside.
- ○ I like variety in the things I do.

| Jobs that match my skills and interests | Are there lots of openings? | Is special training needed? | What is the average hourly wage? |
|---|---|---|---|
|  |  |  |  |
|  |  |  |  |
|  |  |  |  |
|  |  |  |  |
|  |  |  |  |

**How will my criminal record impact my ability to get a job in these fields?**

**Based on my interests and skills, what is my short-term career goal?**

**Based on my interests and skills, what is my long-term career goal?**

**How can I reach my goal? What do I need to do?** List the training or experience you may need.

**Where can I go for help to reach my goal?** List any family, friends, job centers, training programs, reentry programs, or community colleges that can help.

Mapping Your Future, National Edition

# Popular Career Options

In the next few pages, you will find information about popular career options for people with records. These options are just a few of the many options that are available.

## Commercial Drivers

Commercial drivers transport goods, people, and materials. They drive buses, delivery trucks, diesel trucks, and more. Many people who have been incarcerated have had success finding jobs as commercial bus or truck drivers.

| Commercial Driver: Job Facts at a Glance ||
|---|---|
| Wages | $40,000 to $60,000 per year |
| Employment | Very large occupation with lots of openings |
| Education needed | • High school diploma or GED (usually)<br>• Commercial driver's license (CDL) |
| Other requirements | • Good driving record<br>• Strong customer service skills for some positions |

**Prepare in prison:** If you don't already have your GED, get it! You can also study for the road and written tests for your commercial driver's license (CDL) while you're still inside. Look for a copy of the CDL test in your prison's library or resource room.

**Outside of prison:** Here's how you can get started in this field.

- **Apply for a temporary commercial learner's permit.** Speak with the Vehicle Services Department or DMV in your state to find out what you need to do to get a permit and a license. Make sure to mention if you had a CDL in the past or in a different state.
- **Complete CDL training.** If you have not already had training, you may want to take a class at a commercial driver's training facility. Many community colleges offer this training. Some reentry organizations offer programs to help you get your Commercial Driver's License (CDL).
- **Study for the road and written tests.** You can find a copy of the CDL test at your state's DMV or Vehicle Services website to prepare.
- **Get your CDL.** After passing the road and written tests, you will need to pay for the license. You will also need to renew it regularly.

# Construction Jobs

There are many different construction and landscaping careers. People in these careers build and repair homes, buildings, roads, and more. They maintain yards and parks. They install and service heating and cooling (HVAC) systems. They install solar panels. Jobs include:

- Road worker
- Painter
- Heating and air conditioning (HVAC) technician
- Welder
- Solar installer
- General laborer
- Landscaper
- Building maintenance worker and custodian

**Note:** Some construction jobs (such as plumber, electrician, carpenter, or mason) may require an apprenticeship with a trade union. Some of these unions have restrictions about hiring people with criminal records. It's a good idea to check before applying.

| Construction: Job Facts at a Glance | |
|---|---|
| Wages | $40,000 to $70,000 per year, depending on the job |
| Employment | Large occupation, lots of openings |
| Education needed | • High school diploma or GED<br>• Formal training, certificates, or an apprenticeship for some positions<br>• On-the-job training for most positions |
| Other requirements | Driver's license and/or OSHA certification, depending on the position |

**Prepare in prison:** If you have the opportunity, take construction, building maintenance, or horticulture training while in prison. Some prisons may have these programs.

**Outside of prison:** There are lots of ways to get started in a construction field.
- **Some jobs don't require any training at all.** Look for entry level jobs. You'll get training on the job.
- **Community college certificate programs.** Many community colleges offer training in the construction trades.
- **Organizations for women in trades** may offer opportunities to women who are looking to enter either construction or welding. Search online for your city or state and terms like "non-traditional occupations for women" and "programs."

Mapping Your Future, National Edition

# Barbering and Cosmetology

| Barbering and Cosmetology: Job Facts at a Glance ||
|---|---|
| Wages | $34,000 per year |
| Employment | Large occupation, lots of openings |
| Education needed | • High school diploma or GED (for most companies)<br>• On-the-job experience, training, or a license, depending on the job |
| Other requirements | Tools, depending on where you work, though you might be able to share these with a coworker. |

**Prepare in prison:** If you can, get training while in prison.

**Outside of prison:** There are lots of ways to get started.
- **Training.** Search for "Barber College" or "Cosmetology schools" in your community.
- **Self-employment.** If you already have the skills and equipment, you can begin working for friends and build up a client base by word of mouth. Think about what you might be able to offer that others won't. Can you work outside of regular business hours? Are you willing to do house calls? Eventually, you may have to incorporate and pay taxes. You can read more about the process of starting your own business later in this chapter.

# Computer or Information Technology Jobs

There are many jobs for people who like to work with computers. Jobs include help desk technicians, computer network support specialists, computer programmers, computer systems analysts and more. This industry is constantly growing and well paid. Many of these jobs require only a small amount of training and are in great demand.

| Computer or Information Technology: Job Facts at a Glance | |
|---|---|
| Wages | Wages range widely, from about $35,000 for entry level jobs to $80,000+ |
| Employment | Large occupation, lots of openings |
| Education needed | • High school diploma or GED (associate or bachelor's degrees required for some jobs)<br>• Formal training program (such as CompTia A+)<br>• On-the-job training |
| Other requirements | • Strong computer skills<br>• Customer service skills |

**Prepare in prison:** Read anything on the topic that is available. Take advantage of any opportunity to use computers while in prison and learn some basic skills, such as how to use Microsoft Office products like Word or Excel.

**Outside of prison:** There are many different training programs you can take.

- **Libraries, adult education, and community centers** often offer basic computer classes. Goodwill career centers offer training in computer and digital skills, and some classes are online.
- Go to **Northstar** at digitalliteracyassessment.org to test your digital literacy skills and build your skills. You can access classes online or find a Northstar location where you can attend classes. They offer certificates for skills you have mastered.
- Most **community colleges** offer IT certificate programs and degree programs. Many are very affordable.
- If you are a good self learner, try taking computer and IT classes online. **Hackbrite Academy** offers a free online course on Python (a popular programming language). **Skillcrush** teaches other important programming languages like CSS. Programming languages like CSS and HTML create instructions to tell a website what you want it to look like and do. If this is unfamiliar to you, don't worry, you will have the chance to learn. **Edx** and **Coursera** also have a lot of free courses for learning skills like coding or data entry.
- **Columbia University's Justice Through Code** program is a free semester-long intensive coding program for formerly incarcerated people. There are openings each semester, and you can complete the course online. The program helps people find jobs after they complete their training. Check it out here: centerforjustice.columbia.edu/justicethroughcode .

# Dining and Hospitality Jobs

There are many good opportunities in the dining and hospitality industry. Right now, the industry is also seeing major shortages, which means that you might be able to move into a more advanced position more quickly.

There are many different kinds of hospitality companies, and many kinds of roles within those companies. For a typical restaurant job, there is front-of-house, back-of-house, and bar. There are also positions in fast food chains, bars and clubs, hotels, and catering companies.

Many of these jobs require unconventional hours. This may put a strain on your personal relationships, if you are gone most evenings and weekends. These hours can be good if you have kids and want or need to be their primary care provider during the regular working day.

| **Dining and Hospitality: Job Facts at a Glance** ||
|---|---|
| Wages | Wages range widely, from $22,000 for entry level jobs to $80,000+ per year |
| Employment | Large occupation, lots of openings |
| Education needed | • High school diploma or GED<br>• Some jobs may also require:<br>  ○ An associate or bachelor's degree<br>  ○ Formal training programs (Establishments that serve liquor may require certification, for example)<br>  ○ Formal or on-the-job training |
| Other requirements | • Customer service skills<br>• The ability to be calm under pressure, do several things at once, and work well with a team |

**Prepare in prison:** Many facilities have food service programs where you can get experience.

**Outside of prison:**
- Many community colleges and other training programs offer food-services certificates.
- The **COLORS Hospitality Opportunities for Workers** operates a **CHOW Institute** in several major cities in the US and offers comprehensive free training opportunities for restaurant industry personnel. Visit them here: rocunited.org/training-classes .
- **Hospitality Opportunities for People (re)Entering Society (HOPES)** also "connects adults of all ages with current or previous justice-involvement to career opportunities in the restaurant, foodservice, and the hospitality industry." They operate in Massachusetts, Illinois, and Virginia. Request more information using the online form at the bottom of this page: chooserestaurants.org/programs/hopes .

# Human Services and Advocacy

Many EJP alumni (see our introductory chapter, on p. 2) work in human services to help others who have been incarcerated. They are caseworkers, counselors, educators, social workers, mediators, and program managers. They advocate for change and better policies.

We need people who have been incarcerated to help make our systems better! You have experience and wisdom that others can learn from.

Social-services careers can be a meaningful way of moving on and helping others. But they can also be stressful. Be aware that working with others who are struggling may be difficult as you cope with your own challenges and past trauma.

| Human Services and Advocacy: Job Facts at a Glance | |
|---|---|
| Wages | Wages range from $30,000 for entry level jobs to $60,000+ per year |
| Employment | Large occupation, lots of openings |
| Education needed | • High school diploma or GED<br>• Some jobs may also require:<br>   ○ Short-term or on-the-job training<br>   ○ An associate's or bachelor's degree<br>   ○ A driver's license |
| Other requirements | • Strong people skills<br>• Ability to work in stressful situations<br>• Basic computer skills |

**Prepare in prison:** Find ways to get involved in programs that help others. Can you help lead workshops? Tutor others? Be part of a peer support group? Help teach a reentry class? These opportunities will give you a taste of what it's like to work in human services.

Most jobs require some education. If you need it, get your GED and then take college classes if you can. Basic computer classes may also help.

**Outside of prison:**

- **Get involved & volunteer.** Get involved in reentry programs or other services that interest you. Ask the people who are helping you about what they do. Volunteer to help out. Volunteering can lead to job offers. Even if you don't get a job at that organization, they may be able to help connect you to another similar job.
- **Take advantage of leadership and advocacy training.** Reentry organizations often offer training for formerly incarcerated people. Check out our directory of reentry organizations organized by state in the back of this guide.
- **Go to school.** Depending on what your career goal is, you may need an associate or bachelor's degree or an advanced degree. See the Education chapter (on p. 57) for advice.

Mapping Your Future, National Edition

## Self-Employment

Being self-employed has its merits. You can set your own schedule and the money you make is yours (after you pay taxes). You might buy some equipment to do landscaping in your community. You might rent out a small booth to cut people's hair. You might repair people's homes. You might offer computer support. We interviewed David T., a formerly incarcerated individual who started his own business. He offered the following advice.

To get started, you'll need:

1. **A good idea.** Jot down a few ideas on paper first. Ask yourself, what am I good at? What services can I provide? Is there a clear need for this in the community?
2. **Training.** Get all the training you can. Take business or computer classes. You will need strong finance skills, math skills, customer service skills, and more.
3. **Equipment.**
4. **Space for work and storage.** You may be able to work at home or rent a storage shed or small booth.

Seek feedback from others. They might see a challenge or a good idea that you initially overlooked.

*Starting a business can put a strain on your relationships. Talk about your plans with the people you care about. Keep them in loop. Take care to maintain your relationships even when things are busy.*

**—Anonymous**

## Growing Your Idea into a Business

Some people who are self-employed decide to grow their idea into a business by hiring a few more people and getting a more permanent location. You might start your own barbershop, a tutoring business, an HVAC business, or a restaurant.

Starting your own business takes a lot of work. Here are the basic things you'll need to turn your self-employment into a small business:

- **Capital.** You'll need money to start your business.
- **More space.** Maybe you'll rent an office space or garage.
- **Employees.** Who will be part of your team?
- **Marketing plan.** You'll need to be able to attract paying customers.
- **Information.** Do lots of research. What other businesses offer these services? What technologies do they use? How do they get clients?

We recommend that you seek out professional business help. There will be lots of paperwork to manage. You'll have to do taxes and finances for your business. You will likely need to file paperwork with the state to make your business official. You may also want to talk with someone who understands the ins and outs of loans and taxes. Lawyers who advertise experience with incorporation can file your paperwork, but they also charge a fee.

Free resources do exist in communities. Seek out your local business association or Chamber of Commerce to get help.

# Women and Employment

It can be especially hard for women to find jobs after release. When they do find jobs, they often get paid less or work fewer hours. They are more likely to get hired in temp and entry-level jobs, even when they have skills and training for more advanced jobs.

As a woman, here are a few things you may face.

- **Greater discrimination.** People don't expect women to be locked up and often judge them more harshly.
- **Difficulty balancing family and jobs.** Perhaps you have young children, parents, or grandparents you are caring for. It's hard to work a job and care for your family at the same time. It's hard to find childcare.
- **Many of the popular job options for people with criminal records hire mostly men.** You may feel uncomfortable if you are the only woman on the crew.
- **You may feel unsafe at your jobs, or unsafe getting to the job.**

Despite these challenges, we recommend that you approach your job search with patience and hope.

There are barriers that you will face, but many women have found jobs after prison. You can, too.

Here are a few suggestions:

- Get as much education and training as you can while in prison.
- Find reentry and job programs that serve women. They can help you access childcare and get the emotional support you need. The resource directory (see p. 135) lists a few of these programs.
- Be confident! Sometimes women think that they are not qualified. Don't pass up a chance to apply, even if you don't meet all of the requirements.
- Don't be afraid to look for jobs in fields with mostly men, such as construction or IT. In fact, these fields need and want more women! There are free training programs to bring more women into these jobs.
- Be realistic. You will probably have to apply for a number of jobs. You've already dealt with a lot of difficult things, so try to be patient and open minded to the opportunities that arise.

# Look for Jobs

Look for jobs you think you could be good at. What experience, education, and training do they require? What strengths would you bring? Is the job a good fit for your skills?

Even if you don't meet all of the requirements, think about applying anyway. Don't sell yourself short! Be confident in your skills and abilities. Sometimes, you can get the training you need on the job.

**Network.** Networking is the best way to find a job. Talk to family, friends, acquaintances, and professionals. They may not have a job for you right now, but they could have advice. Maybe they know someone else who is hiring.

**Search online.** These days, many people find jobs through websites like monster.com, careerbuilder.com, and snagajob.com, and indeed.com. These websites collect job postings from employer websites, job boards, and more. Sites like these are best for finding work with large employers. For smaller employers, you may want to look at company websites. Often, you will find a link to "Current Jobs," "Careers," or "Employment" on the home page. The website "Jobs that Hire Felons" has a long list of companies whose hiring policies include people with a background: jobsthathirefelons.org . Honest Jobs is another: www.honestjobs.com .

When searching for a job online, be careful to avoid scams. Scammers may request money or ask for information like your date of birth, Social Security number, or debit/credit card number. We advise that you never give out this personal information on the internet.

☆ Need to use a computer? Visit your public library.

**Attend a job fair** to meet employers, recruiters, and schools. You may learn about a new field or opportunity that you didn't think of.

☆ Keep a record of all the places you have applied: online applications, visits made in person, initial phone calls, follow-up phone calls, interviews.

Submit **application forms.** The purpose of a job application form is to get an interview. Most hiring managers will review your application for 15 to 30 seconds. They'll want to see a form that's neat and complete.

Many job applications need to be filled out online. If you don't have access to a home computer, visit a local library or community center.

If you will be filling out a paper job application at a job site, bring notes about previous jobs and training, including employment dates, job titles, and former employer contact info. This is better than trying to remember the details and making mistakes.

### Tips for filling out job applications

- **List your past jobs and describe what you did.** What skills did you develop? What things did you do during your shift?
- **Focus on what you have to offer.** Downplay the negatives.
- **List work experience from your personal life.** Were you a caregiver for your siblings, children, parents, or grandparents? What skills did you develop? Did you learn to communicate, resolve conflicts, manage people's health, or take care of finances?
- **Consider the skills they are looking for.** If they want good customer service skills, explain how you worked with customers in your past jobs.
- **Use examples from your personal life to explain your passion for this work.** Maybe when you were a young child, you took care of your sick grandmother. This inspired you to become an excellent home health aid.
- **Do not list your wages from past employment.** Instead, write "will discuss at the interview."
- **We suggest you list the jobs you held while incarcerated.** You gained relevant experience and skills. For in-prison jobs, you can list your employer as the state where you were incarcerated.
- **If they ask you for your "Reason for Leaving" give a positive reason, if possible, even if you were fired or let go.** Here are a few positive reasons for leaving:
    - You relocated (you can say this if you left because you went to prison or were transferred)
    - You wanted a career change
    - You became a full-time student
    - The work was seasonal
    - You wanted to advance or make more money
- In some states, most employers are not allowed to ask about felonies on job applications. Some still do. **If they ask, "Have you ever been convicted of a felony?" we recommend that you check "Yes." Write, "Will discuss at interview."** If you lie, you may get the job, but you could get fired later if they find out.
- **The application may ask you for references, people who can vouch for you.** These should not be family members. Be sure to ask people if they are willing to be your reference before writing their names down. Good potential references include:
    - Former or current employers
    - Supervisors
    - Teachers
    - Social workers
    - Religious leaders
    - People you volunteer with

**Resumes and cover letters.** Many job applications require a resume and cover letter. A resume maps out past jobs, your skills, and your interests. Your cover letter is an actual letter from you to the employer. It tells a short story about who you are—why you want the job, why you are a good fit, and what's important to you. Keep your letter to one page.

Writing good resumes and cover letters takes time. Examples of resumes and cover letters can be found in our forms section (see p. 159). Here are a few online resources:

- hbr.org/2014/02/how-to-write-a-cover-letter
- owl.purdue.edu/owl/job_search_writing

*I thought I'd be prepared because I had my resume in hand. As it turns out, you need several resumes, adjusted to different jobs, and the ability to write cover sheets on the fly.*

—Pablo

**Interviews.** Once you've submitted your job application, wait to be contacted. Hopefully, they will be interested in interviewing you. Most applications do not lead to interviews. Be patient. Continue to apply to other jobs until you have a job offer.

Many job seekers are nervous about interviews. They want to say the right things and make a good impression. Here are a few tips:

- **Practice.** Indeed.com has a list of common interview questions that you can practice with a friend, counselor, or family member: www.indeed.com/career-advice/interviewing/top-interview-questions-and-answers .
- **What to bring.** Bring your resume and contact information for your references. Bring copies of work licenses, your driving record, and your Social Security or immigration cards, too. Bring a pen and notebook to write down information.
- **Arrive 10 to 15 minutes early.** This shows you are responsible and eager to be there.
- **Wear nice clothes.** Wear something a bit more formal than what you would wear for the job.
- Consider your body language. Make good eye contact, stand/sit tall, and smile.
- **Test your equipment.** If your interview is online, test your video and internet connection beforehand. Make sure you're in a quiet place without disruptions.
- **Come prepared to ask the employer questions.** Here are some examples:
    - What is the organization's plan for the next five years?
    - How would I be evaluated, and in what timeframes? By whom?
    - What are the day-to-day responsibilities of this job?
    - What computer equipment and software do you use?
    - When will a decision be made about this position?

*Interview tips? Look good, smell good, speak good.*

—David T.

**Talking about your criminal record.** You may have a hard time answering questions about your criminal record. Here are a few tips to increase your chance of getting hired:

- **Own it.** "At that time I was making some bad choices and I was convicted of [state your offense]." Address any concerns they have.
- **Redirect.** Steer the interview back to your skills and what you bring to the job. "I can see why that might concern you. But that was several years ago. Since then, I have had a solid work record. I come to work on time. I am a hard worker and quick learner."
- **Explain.** If your felony conviction is not related to the job you are applying for, you might say, "Yes, I was convicted of a felony, but it was not job related."
- **Keep it positive.** Talk about your current activities and future career goals. Mention education and job training, community work, and other activities. "I thought a lot about where my life was going, and I decided to make some changes."
- **Encourage the employer.** Remind them how much you want the job. "I am a good worker and I want to work, I just need an opportunity to prove my skills to an employer."

*If you're scared to tell an employer, hey, I've been to prison, just tell them. What's the worst thing they can do? Say no, we're not going to hire you. And you go to the next door. Knock on the next door. Say hey, are you hiring?*

— Tony C.

## Advice from an Employer

We reached out to Tanja, an employer who has hired many people who have been incarcerated. In the interview below, Tanja explains what employers are looking for. She gives advice about how to talk about your criminal history with employers.

### What are the most important qualities you look for in a job candidate?

For me, the most important quality is reliability. I also appreciate it when people are eager to learn and respond well to constructive feedback. The fit between the person and the position is also critical.

### How much do you need to say about your criminal background?

I think it really depends on the position. It is a mistake to come in and tell me your whole life. That is too much too soon. But being super vague will make me wonder if you are trying to hide something. For me, honesty is critical. I let people know I am not here to judge, and as far as I am concerned, they have done their time. What I care about is the present and the future. Can they do this job now? How much training and supervision will they need? What are their skills?

### What impresses you about candidates?

I am usually impressed when I see someone who has done their homework. They know what the position is, they Googled the company and they know what we are looking for. It is ideal to tailor your history to the position and capitalize on your skills. Link these skills to the job announcement and tell me how these skills will be used to help me. Also demonstrate enthusiasm for what the company does. If it is the restaurant industry, tell me how much you enjoy the food and why. If you do not enjoy the food, find something you like about the company and share that with me.

### What questions should the interviewee ask the employer?

Do your homework about my company, the job description, and ask me questions as if you had the position. Ask for details about logistics: How many hours, what days and times do you need me? What qualities are you looking for in a worker? What would a typical day be like on the job? What are the opportunities for growth? Do you offer training, and if so, how does that work? Who will be my supervisor? What is their management style? These questions will make me believe you are serious about the job. In my case, I provide reentry services. I want to see you know the reentry process and that you are passionate about this issue.

### What questions can they expect in an interview?

- Why are you applying for this job now?
- What is your availability? Convince me that you will be available and reliable. Make sure you can make the work schedule work.
- What are your best skills? What skills would you like to develop?
- What were you doing before? This question can be tricky if you have a big gap in your resume. If you were just released, be honest, but capitalize on the skills you have that make you right for this position. Point me to your references and how they will assure me that you are worth taking a chance on.

# Your Legal Rights

## Equal Employment Laws

The Equal Employment Opportunity Commission (EEOC) is a federal agency that administers and enforces civil rights laws for the workplace in all states. Their guidelines address the following issues:

**Background Check.** Employers who wish to do a background check must also do the following:

- Get your written consent ahead of time
- Tell you if they plan to use the report for employment decisions
- Give you a copy of the report before taking harmful action (like not hiring or firing you)
- Inform you of your right to review and dispute the report

**Employment Denial.** In order to legally deny you

employment based on a conviction, employers must consider:

- The nature and gravity of the criminal offense or conduct
- How much time has passed since the offense or sentence
- The nature of the job (where it is performed, supervision, and interaction with others)

If there isn't a direct relationship between the job and your offense, employers cannot legally use the offense to deny you employment. For example, it would be legal for a bank to deny someone convicted of credit card fraud or theft. But, it would most likely not be legal for them to deny someone who was convicted of drug possession.

Employers can still choose candidates with more or better experience, but irrelevant criminal history should not be a deciding factor. If you believe you have been discriminated against, you can file a complaint with the EEOC by mail, by telephone (call 800-669-4000), or in person at an EEOC office: www.eeoc.gov .

## Certificate of Rehabilitation

A criminal record can prevent you from getting a license in certain fields, including education, transit, and childcare. You may be able to get a Certificate of Rehabilitation. The certificate allows you to apply for jobs that require these licenses. It does not remove any offenses from your record, but it may allow you to get the license you need. See the Legal Matters chapter (on p. 92).

## Work Opportunity Tax Credits

If employers seem reluctant to hire you, you may want to tell them about the Work Opportunity Tax Credit. Employers who hire people with convictions receive a tax credit of up to 40 percent of the employee's yearly wages. The tax credit is only for employers who hire people who have left prison within the last year. You could direct them to this website: www.dol.gov/agencies/eta/wotc .

## Federal Bonding Program

When interviewing for a job, you may also want to tell the employer about the Federal Bonding Program. It is an insurance policy that protects employers from employee dishonesty or theft. They offer six months of free insurance for employees with past convictions. Learn more here: bonds4jobs.com . Some states have bonding programs as well.

## Ban the Box

Some counties, cities, and states have laws that prevent employers from conducting criminal background checks until after an interview is conducted. This law is called "Ban the Box" because it prohibits employers from asking you to check a box on your application saying you've had a criminal conviction. These states have Ban the Box laws: California, Colorado, Connecticut, Hawaii, Illinois, Massachusetts, Maryland, Minnesota, New Jersey, New Mexico, Oregon, Rhode Island, Washington, and Vermont. Many other states and even more counties and cities have Ban the Box rules for government and city jobs. If you live in a place with a Ban the Box law and an employer violates this rule, you can submit a complaint against them.

The details of Ban the Box laws change from place to place. To find out more about your local protections and how to lodge a complaint, contact a local re-entry program. (See the resource directory on p. 135).

## Conflicts and Safety

If you are being harassed or discriminated against because of your race, gender identity, or sexual orientation, your civil rights are being violated. If you are comfortable speaking honestly where you are working, you can speak to Human Resources about what you have experienced. Sometimes it's better to seek help elsewhere.

There are resources that can support you. If you have been sexually harassed, you can contact the National Sexual Assault Hotline at (800) 656-4673 for personal support. They can help you file a complaint.

It is a good idea to get a lawyer before starting a lawsuit. There are pro bono (free) lawyers who can help—see the Legal Matters chapter (on p. 92). If you are ready to file a complaint on your own, you may do so at the **US Department of Justice Civil Rights Division.**

If you are working in a place that is unsafe, you can file a complaint with the Occupational Safety and Health Administration (OSHA) by calling (800) 321-6742 or going to www.osha.gov/workers/file-complaint . If you think that something may be unsafe, but don't have proof, you may notify your employer in writing. If they do not resolve the issue, you may then file a complaint with OSHA.

Of course, it is hard to address these problems if you are in an insecure position and need to keep your job. If you are able to talk to a lawyer, they might be able to offer helpful advice. See the Legal Matters chapter for more information (p. 92).

# Unemployment Benefits

Most people who leave prison are not able to get unemployment benefits, but you may be eligible if you had been working for a while before you went to prison. You must have lost your job through no fault of your own (by being laid off, for example), and you need to have made at least $1,600 in the 12 months before you filed your claim. You cannot receive unemployment directly after you return home if you lost your previous job due to your incarceration or if you were in prison for more than twelve months.

Get more information from your state's department of unemployment benefits. In Illinois, you can check at the Department of Employment Security office or your local workNet Center. In other states, search for "department of unemployment benefits" and the name of your state. You can also look in the directory (see p. 135) for local reentry organizations that can direct you to local employment resources.

# Education

A lot of people think about going back to school after they leave prison. Going to school helps you learn more about the world. It can also help you meet new people and get better jobs.

This chapter has information about different education programs, like:

- Adult Basic Education (ABE), GED, and High School Equivalency Programs
- Vocational Training and Apprenticeships
- College
- Paying for Your Education

It's never too late to go to school or college. Learning can even make you feel happier and more fulfilled. You can go to school part-time or full-time. If you are still in prison, you may be able to take classes before you leave.

## ABE, GED, and High School Equivalency Programs

Adult Basic Education (ABE) programs can help you get better at reading, writing, math, listening, and speaking. You can usually find ABE programs at adult schools, career centers, libraries, and community colleges. They are free or cost only a little. Agencies like Kaplan and ELS Language Centers also offer ABE, but they charge more money.

ABE programs can also help you learn English or prepare for your state's high school equivalent test.

The General Education Development (GED) test is the most common high-school-equivalency test. GEDs and similar tests work like a high school diploma. If you did not graduate from high school, you can take this test and it will count on your resume as a diploma. Many jobs require that you have a GED, a high school diploma, or another high-school-equivalency certificate.

If you don't have one of these yet, try to get one. The test will have questions about things you would learn in high school. You can register online to take the GED test at ged.com . You will probably take the test on a computer at an official GED testing site. If your state doesn't offer the GED, search for "high school equivalency" and your state's name.

The GED is not an easy test. You will probably need to study. A lot of places have free preparation programs that can help you get ready:

- Community colleges
- Adult learning centers (find one using this directory: www.nld.org)
- Online study programs
- American Job Centers (find one here: www.dol.gov/general/topic/training/onestop )

A lot of programs will let you sign up at any time. They can also give you a study plan to help you get better in harder subjects.

Do you need help learning how to use new technology? Go to **Northstar** at digitalliteracyassessment.org to get help. They have online classes and in-person ones at different locations. They will give you certificates when you gain new skills.

Mapping Your Future, National Edition

# Vocational Training and Apprenticeships

Vocational programs help you learn how to do a job. They can teach you things like welding, car repair, plumbing, and more. You can take these classes at community and technical colleges as well as trade schools.

A lot of prisons have vocational classes. Take them if you can. Vocational classes help you get some experience and see if you like the work. Once you leave, you can get an entry-level position or an apprenticeship. Apprenticeships help you get training and experience. You'll also get paid through an apprenticeship. Apprenticeships are usually offered through trade unions.

The American Job Center is a good place to look. Start here: usa.gov/find-a-job .

For more information on apprenticeship programs, go to www.apprenticeship.gov/apprenticeship-job-finder .

*Consider seeking simple certifications, like CDL, sanitation, limo driver, or forklift.*

**—Earl W.**

| Degree type | Information |
|---|---|
| Vocational certificates | • Certificates that prepare you for specific jobs or tasks<br>• Varied amounts of time required<br>• Granted by community colleges, technical and trade schools, or workforce programs |
| Associate's degree | • Two-year degree<br>• Granted by a community college, university, or technical school |
| Bachelor's degree (often written as B.S. or B.A.) | • Four-year degree<br>• Granted by a college or university |
| Master's degree | • Two- or three-year degree<br>• Completed after earning a bachelor's degree<br>• Typically requires research |
| Doctor of Philosophy (often called a doctorate or doctoral degree and written as Ph.D.) | • Typically takes four to six years<br>• Completed after earning a bachelor's or master's degree<br>• Highest academic degree |
| Professional degrees | • Required to practice in certain professions, like medicine and law<br>• Completed after earning a bachelor's degree |

# College

## Community college

If you haven't been in school for a while, you might want to start at community college. Community colleges are inexpensive and offer many different classes. A lot of them offer programs where you can get a GED and college credit at the same time. Community colleges usually offer associate degrees, certificate programs, and workforce training.

If you start at a community college and decide you want to continue your education at a four-year college, you can usually apply your community-college classes toward your degree at the four-year college. This is called "transferring your credits" (see "Four-year college," below).

## Four-year college/university

Many people who want to earn a four-year bachelor's degree start by attending community college. They then transfer to a four-year college or university to finish. This saves money because community college costs less than four-year schools.

You must earn a certain number of credits to get a bachelor's degree. Some credits have to be in general subjects, like science, math, and history. If you finish these credits at a community college and then transfer to a school that offers a four-year degree, your credits can transfer too. Make sure to check that your new school will count your transfer credits.

To learn more, visit the websites of the schools you're interested in, or you can call, email, or visit an admissions counselor or academic advisor at these schools.

> What's the difference between a college and university? Both offer bachelor's degrees. Colleges are often smaller and private. Universities are larger, and offer graduate degrees. They are often public and do more than just offering classes. They engage in research and often have a large athletics department.

## Where should you apply?

Deciding where to go may take some time. Think about what kind of degree you want and what kind of college or university you want to go to. Research colleges online or at the local library. Almost all colleges have websites where you can learn about their price, academic programs, non-academic activities, the town where they are located, and many other things. You can also call colleges' admissions offices to receive this information.

## Applying for College

### Step 1: Get the application

For almost all colleges, you will apply on their websites. A librarian at a public library can provide help.

### Step 2: Gather your information

To apply for college you will probably need:
- Your Social Security number
- A state driver's license or identification card
- Your dates of high school and any completed college courses
- GED results or unopened transcripts from your high school and/or college, whichever you completed most recently.
- Some four-year colleges will also ask for ACT or SAT test scores. (See Step 3, below.) You can find specific application requirements on each college's website.

Some applications may ask about your record. If you tell them you have been convicted of a felony, some schools will ask for more information. Just because they are asking for the information doesn't mean you will be rejected. Different schools have different policies about backgrounds. You can also ask to speak with an admissions counselor about this.

### Step 3: Take the SAT or ACT exam

Is this your first time applying for college? Some four-year colleges require you to take the ACT or SAT college-entrance exam. Check the college's website for specific application requirements. If you are required to take an exam, an admissions counselor can give you more information. It helps to study. You can buy study guides or get them from your public library. Khan Academy offers online SAT test prep for free at www.khanacademy.org/sat .

### Step 4: Complete the essay

Most four-year colleges require a "statement of purpose" or "personal statement" essay. This might be the hardest part of the application, but these essays let you shine. Make sure you put your goals in the essay. Ask a few people you trust to carefully check your essay for mistakes. Ask them to also make sure you sound purposeful and confident.

### Step 5: Submit the application

You'll probably hear from a community college within a few weeks. They'll let you know by phone or letter if you've been accepted. Four-year colleges and universities can take longer. If you have questions, contact the school's admissions office.

# Paying for Your Education

Paying for your education can be hard. Below we describe how you can get money for college.

**Free tuition programs.** Some colleges offer free tuition if you meet certain income requirements. Check with the college you are interested in attending. Veterans can also get money for college. See studentaid.gov/understand-aid/types/military .

You'll also need to pay for living expenses, books, and fees.

### Financial Aid: FAFSA

Do you need financial aid for college? The Free Application for Federal Student Aid (FAFSA) is the place to start.

**How do I apply?** You can find the FAFSA online at How do I apply? You can find the FAFSA online at www.fafsa.gov , or you can request a paper copy by calling (800) 433-3243. Applying for federal student aid is free. But it can be complicated. If you're worried or have questions, ask for help. Colleges' financial aid offices can help you over the phone, through email, or in person.

**When is it due?** Check on the form to see when it is due for your state. You should also ask your college when it is due. They might have an earlier deadline. Look at the school's website or call their financial aid office. Turn in your FAFSA as soon as you can, because some financial aid runs out fast. If you can, turn in your FAFSA while you're in prison. That way everything will be ready in time for you to start school.

**What kind of aid will I get?** The aid you get will depend on how much money you make and the cost of your school. Your aid package may include the following:

- **Pell Grants** are government grants that are based on financial need.
- **Scholarships** can come from the college or from other organizations. Ask your financial aid office about scholarships. Scholarship information can also be found at public libraries and online.
- **Federal student loans** have lower interest rates than banks, and you won't have to start paying them back until after you graduate. But you will have to pay them back. Think carefully about how you will repay your loans. Your loans will impact your decisions about money and jobs.
- **Work study positions** allow you to pay for college by working for the school. You can say you are interested in work-study when you fill out the FAFSA. Work-study is a good way to make money and get more work experience. They are often offered first-come, first-served because there might not be enough positions for everyone who would like to work.

Your financial aid package may include several kinds of aid. You don't have to accept the whole package. You can choose the parts that work for you. For example, you could accept a grant but not a loan. Reach out to the office if you have questions or want help understanding your package.

**Can I get federal student aid if I have a criminal record?** In most cases, yes. There are two exceptions. You cannot get federal student aid if:

- You were convicted of a drug offense (a misdemeanor or felony) while you were receiving financial aid in the past. This might not affect you if enough time has passed, or if you have completed drug treatment. Drug convictions from before you started college shouldn't have any effect. Ask your school financial aid staff for more information about this.
- You were subject to an involuntary civil commitment after completing a period of incarceration for a forcible or non-forcible sexual offense. If this is the case, you cannot receive Pell Grants.

For more information on financial aid for those with a felony conviction, see studentaid.gov/understand-aid/eligibility/requirements/criminal-convictions . It would also be helpful to speak with a financial aid officer at the schools you are applying to.

> If a grant, loan, or scholarship offer sounds too good to be true, it probably is. There are many for-profit companies that take advantage of people who are looking to go to college. Applying for financial aid should be free, and you should research the agency or company before applying.

Remember to keep copies of all applications and related paperwork in your portfolio.

☆ For a useful guide to getting your education after incarceration, see "How to Earn Your Degree and Get Hired After Incarceration." You can access it here: bestaccreditedcolleges.org/resources/formerly-incarcerated-education-career-guide .

# Resources for College Students

**Tutoring centers.** Do you need extra help with your classes? A lot of people do. Many college campuses offer free tutoring to their students. Your tuition pays for such services, so be sure to get your money's worth.

**Mentoring and student support programs.** Some colleges offer mentoring programs to new students. College mentors are students or people who give support to new students. Some colleges even have mentor programs for people with records!

**Career center.** Most colleges have career centers that can help you find a job while you are in school and when you graduate. Career centers also offer help with resume writing, getting ready for interviews, and more. Again, your tuition pays for these services, so use them!

**The Formerly Incarcerated College Graduates Network** is an amazing resource! Build community, find support from peers, share resources, find job openings, advocate for policy change, and share your story. Visit: www.ficgn.org .

...............  ...............

*A full-time, work-study student with [SNAP] benefits can bring in $800 a month plus free transportation. That is a game changer.*

—**Earl W.**

.................................................

Mapping Your Future, National Edition

# Health

When you leave prison, you will need to manage your own health. This can be a welcome change, but can also be stressful. There are many different options for health insurance. There are many kinds of clinics, hospitals, and doctors to choose from. There are paperwork, applications, and bills to figure out. Be willing to ask for help from family and friends as you figure things out.

In this section, we cover:
- Health Insurance
- Dental and Vision Care
- Doctor Visits
- Pharmacy
- COVID-19
- HIV/AIDS and Other Diseases

See also the Trauma and Mental Health chapter (on p. 68) and the Substance Use chapter (on p. 76).

 ## Health Insurance

Medical care can be very costly! Health insurance can help pay for doctor's visits, medications, vaccines, laboratory tests, and emergencies. Health insurance can also be expensive, but medical care can cost hundreds or thousands of dollars if you are not insured.

**Getting care if you are uninsured.** If you don't have health insurance but need care, there are public and community health programs and clinics that offer free or low-cost services.

These community clinics provide:
- Vaccinations and immunizations
- Full physicals
- Nutrition and food stamp programs
- STD screening, cancer screening, HIV/AIDS services
- Dental care
- Pregnancy and maternity assistance
- Programs to quit smoking
- Hearing tests and eye exams

Find a public health program or clinic at freeclinicdirectory.org .

### Medicaid and Medicare

Medicaid and Medicare are federal programs that offer assistance with healthcare costs.

- **Medicaid** delivers assistance to people who earn less than the Medicaid income limit in their state. Most hospitals and health clinics accept Medicaid payments.
- **Medicare** assists people who are 65 years old or older

To see if you qualify, visit www.healthcare.gov .

You can apply to Medicaid or Medicare one of four ways:

1. **Apply in prison** before you leave, if you can. Talk to your counselor or clinical services.
2. **Apply online.** Most states have their own online applications, but you can begin here: www.benefits.gov/categories/Healthcare and Medical Assistance .
3. **Apply in person** at a hospital, a Department of Human Services center, or another place that offers case management.

4. **Apply by mail or fax.** You can call your state's Department of Human Services to mail you an application. Complete the application and mail or fax it in.

Before applying you need to have a few documents ready:

- **Income verification.** This could be pay stubs, a financial-aid award letter, a written statement from your employer, or a copy of your check stub showing your total income before taxes.
- **Your Social Security number**
- **Proof of residency.** Any official document showing your address and name together will work.

When you fill out your Medicaid application, you can also apply for other benefits, such as SNAP (Supplemental Nutrition Assistance Program) and TANF (Temporary Assistance for Needy Families). See Resources to Meet your Basic Needs (on p. 32) for more information about these and other assistance programs.

If you receive Medicaid benefits (or benefits from any of these other programs), report any changes to your income or dependent status as soon as possible. If you begin making more money than is allowed, you may no longer qualify for these programs. You will start to lose parts of your tax refund on a monthly basis. You can report these changes to your local food stamp authority (often called the Department of Human Services or Department of Health and Human Services depending on the state).

## Other Health Insurance Options

If you do not qualify for Medicaid or Medicare, there are a few other options.

- Your state may have its own low-cost health insurance program. Contact your local Department of Human Services office for more information.
- You may be able to get insurance through your employer. If you are in college, you may be able to get insurance through your school. If you are under 25, you may still be able to be on your parents' insurance.
- If you cannot get Medicare, Medicaid, or insurance through your employer, the Healthcare Marketplace may be an option. It is a federal program that works with health insurance companies to offer plans for individuals and families. After you are released from prison, you have 60 days to enroll. You can also enroll right after major life events or during the annual open enrollment period. Go to www.healthcare.gov or call (800) 318-2596 to talk to someone who can help you complete your application.

*You have to be in charge of everything yourself. You're not going to get called in later for a physical. The onus falls on you.*

—**Pablo**

*Go to a community medical center. You can get a free full physical when you get out of prison. We have to make sure there are no underlying conditions that we aren't aware of.*

—**Joe Joe**

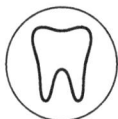

# Dental and Vision Care

Get your teeth cleaned and examined regularly. Oral health is important for your overall health. Teeth problems can lead to bigger health problems in the future. Get your eyes checked regularly, too. If you have vision problems like glaucoma, cataracts, or retinal tears, it is especially important to take care of your eyes.

Dental and vision are not always included in health insurance plans, so think about your needs and check for each plan before you enroll. There may be separate dental or vision plans that you can get.

If your insurance plan does not cover vision, you may want to buy a separate plan for eye care. Health insurance plans that offer vision care often cover yearly eye exams and some of the cost of glasses and contacts. Medicare covers eye exams, and Medicaid covers vision care for children.

### Low-Cost Dental and Eye Care

Here are some low-cost options for dental care:

- Go to www.nidcr.nih.gov/health-info/finding-dental-care to find low-cost dental care.
- Find a dental school in your area by visiting this website: www.ada.org/en/coda/find-a-program . Dental students can do dental work for a lower cost while gaining experience.
- Some dentists will accept Medicaid payments—ask them to find out.

There are several programs that offer free or low-cost eye exams and glasses:

- Walmart and Target have stores with eye shops where you can get an exam and glasses for cheap.
- Eyecare America offers eye exams: www.aao.org/eyecare-america
- InfantSEE offers free eye exams for 6-to-12-month-old babies: www.infantsee.org
- Sight for Students offers glasses for children: (888) 290-4964
- New Eyes offers a free glasses program: (973) 376-4903
- Zennioptical.com and www.goggles4u.com offer frames starting at around $10. You will need to provide a prescription from your eye doctor.

# Doctor Visits

It's a good idea to establish a regular relationship with your doctor (often called your "primary care provider," or PCP). Most health insurance plans require you to pick a primary care provider. This person will serve as your "medical home" and is usually a family physician, nurse practitioner, physician's assistant, or internal medicine physician. Having regular visits with a primary care provider is the best way to manage your health. Unless it's an emergency, go see this person instead of going to the emergency room or an urgent-care clinic. This will save you money and time and keep you healthy.

A primary care physician can give you a full physical exam, perform lab work, and provide prescription renewals. It is recommended that you have a full physical at least once a year and complete routine exams. Below are some age-based recommendations for routine exams.

# Routine Exams That Can Keep You Healthy

| Age | Men | Women |
|---|---|---|
| 18-39 | Blood pressure, cholesterol, flu shot, syphilis screen, TDAP shot, HPV shot, chlamydia/gonorrhea, HIV, skin exam | Blood pressure, cholesterol, flu shot, TDAP shot, HPV shot, breast exam, after 21 PAP test, chlamydia/gonorrhea, HIV, skin exam |
| 40-64 | Blood pressure, blood sugar, colonoscopy (over 50), stool test, flu shot, shingles shot (over 60), prostate screen (over 50), lung cancer screen (only if you smoke), skin exam | Blood pressure, blood sugar, colonoscopy (over 50), stool test, flu shot, shingles shot (over 60), breast screen, mammogram (over 40), lung cancer screen (only if you smoke), postmenopausal bone screening, PAP test, pelvic, HPV, skin exam |
| 65+ | Blood pressure, blood sugar, cholesterol, colonoscopy until 75, hearing test, aneurysm screen (if smoker), prostate and lung screening (only if you have risk factors), pneumonia shot x2, skin exam | Blood pressure, blood sugar, cholesterol, colonoscopy until 75, hearing test, mammogram until 75, bone screening, PAP test until 65, pneumonia shot x2, skin exam |

Your primary care provider can also refer you to specialists for some health concerns. One way to contact your primary care physician is by signing up through your hospital network's online portal. This will allow you to access your medical records, send messages to your doctor, and schedule appointments.

*Going to the office of my primary care physician was actually a pleasant experience. It was nothing like it was on the inside.*

—**Pablo**

 # Pharmacy

Some insurance plans will help you pay for expensive medical prescriptions, while others do not. If you are having trouble paying for your prescriptions, here are a few options:
- Ask your doctor or pharmacist if there is a generic version of the drugs you need. Generic drugs are much less expensive.
- Go to Goodrx.com to compare prices of prescription medications. It tells you where you can go for the best price.
- Stores like Target, Walmart, Costco, and Sam's Club often have special programs where you can get cheap generic drugs ($4 for 30-day quantity or $10 for a 90-day quantity).
- Go to www.rxassist.org to find out if the medication you need is offered for free to people who qualify.

Mapping Your Future, National Edition

# COVID-19

On May 11, 2023, the Department of Health and Human Services declared the end of the public health emergency that is COVID-19, but this doesn't mean COVID-19 is gone. The virus continues to mutate and new variants still arise. It's important to continue to protect ourselves against COVID-19 and other illnesses.

Here are the most important things to keep yourself and others healthy:

1. **Get a vaccine.** Even if you aren't at high risk, a vaccine will protect you and those around you. The vaccines have been tested on thousands of people. They are safe. They effectively prevent serious COVID-19 infection. You should get a vaccine even if you have already had COVID-19. You can get a free vaccine at most pharmacies. Consider getting a flu shot, too.
2. **Get booster shots.** Keep track of your vaccination dates. Ask a pharmacist or your doctor when you will be eligible for a follow-up shot (a booster). When you are eligible for a booster, get one. They will help keep you safe.
3. **Wear a mask if you are at all sick to keep the people around you safe.** If you are worried about getting sick, wear a mask when you are around a lot of people. More and more people these days are wearing masks just to stay healthy. Masks can be purchased at any pharmacy or grocery store. A lot of places offer free masks.
4. **Pay attention to infection levels.** If a lot of people are getting sick, it's good to be more cautious.
5. **Isolate if you are sick or have been around someone who is sick.**
6. **Wash your hands** often and avoid touching your face.

## If You Get Sick

COVID-19 can look like a lot of different illnesses. The most common symptoms are fever, cough, and shortness of breath. You might feel tired or achy. You might vomit or have diarrhea. Some show no symptoms while others become very sick and end up in the hospital on a ventilator.

If you have mild symptoms, you can treat the virus at home. Rest, drink plenty of water, take acetaminophen (Tylenol) for the fever and drink warm tea with honey for a cough. Stay away from others as much as possible.

> **Emergency Warning Signs**
>
> Do you have trouble breathing, pain or pressure in the chest, or confusion? Are you so sleepy it is difficult to wake you? Go to a hospital emergency room right away or call 9-1-1.
>
> If you think you might have COVID, you can get a COVID-19 test at many places. Call 2-1-1.

.....................................................

# HIV/AIDS and Other Diseases

Being in prison increases the risk of getting some diseases. After release from prison, you should be tested for HIV, Hepatitis C (HCV), Hepatitis B (HBV), and tuberculosis. HIV, HBV, and HCV can be detected by a blood test. Tuberculosis can be tested by blood or by a skin test. Locations for HIV testing can be found by using the CDC's HIV Test Locator at: www.cdc.gov/std/hiv .

If you test positive for HIV or another serious disease, know that you can still live a long and meaningful life. You should make an appointment to see a healthcare provider to stay healthy and possibly begin treatments.

You should still be cautious if the test comes back negative. It is possible that the tests missed the virus. To be safe, request a second test after two weeks.

## What Does Having HIV Mean?

HIV is a virus that spreads by attacking and killing healthy cells in the body. This happens all over the body, destroying cells or forcing them to create new infected cells.

HIV targets immune system cells known as T-cells. T-cells fight off infection by killing cells that have been infected by germs. As more T-cells start dying, the immune system is open to attack. If the number of T-cells drops too low, the risk of infection increases and can lead to AIDS. When someone has AIDS, their immune system becomes too weak to fight off other infections. If untreated, people can die of AIDS.

Fortunately, people who have HIV today can live long and productive lives as long as they stay on top of their infection. To do so, they need daily medication, regular testing and doctor visits, and healthy lifestyle changes (like exercise, stopping smoking, getting enough sleep, etc.).

Sometimes HIV testing is offered as part of the prison release process. We suggest you take advantage of this free testing, as knowing your status is very important.

## Risk

The most common way for HIV to be transmitted is through sexual contact. Infected and untreated mothers are also able to pass it on to their children. Avoid contact with blood, semen, or vaginal fluid from sexual partners who are HIV-positive. Do not share needles or syringes, and make sure to use protection (condoms) for any sexual contact.

Know the risk of spreading HIV to a sexual partner who is not HIV positive. Being treated with antiretroviral medications can reduce your chances of transmitting HIV to a partner. Taking antiretroviral medications regularly lowers the levels of HIV in your blood. This does not mean that the virus is completely gone, so take precautions and use condoms even though the risk of transmission is low. If you do not have HIV but are in a relationship with someone who does, you can take PrEP (Pre-Exposure Prophylaxis), which reduces the risk of being infected.

There are also certain sexual activities that can increase your chances of transmitting HIV. For more information about HIV transmission and risk factors, visit: www.hiv.gov/hiv-basics .

*Make sure that there's not something wrong with you that they didn't test for or detect while you were inside. When I first got home, they ran all these tests. I got called a few days later asking if I could come in again to see the doctor. When I came in, she went over the results, and she said, it doesn't look bad but you have chronic kidney disease. She wrote me a referral to go see a kidney specialist and she gave me some literature to read about the disease and how I could have gotten it.*

—Shaun W.

 ## Reflect

1. What are my healthcare needs? Do I have any needs that might require special health care?

2. How will I get access to that healthcare? What are my insurance options?

3. What steps can I take to stay healthy?

4. Who is the doctor or nurse practitioner I can call if I need help? When is my first appointment?

Mapping Your Future, National Edition

# Trauma and Mental Health

Know that if you are struggling with trauma or mental health difficulties, you are not alone. Most people who are incarcerated have experienced trauma. Most also struggle with their mental health. Being in prison can trigger mental health difficulties or make them worse. Your time in prison may cause trauma that affects your mental health long after you leave.

If you have mental health difficulties, **seek treatment as soon as you are released.** Reentry is hard. Mental health difficulties can make reentry much harder. Sadly, people who do not get treatment are more likely to return to prison.

There are mental health professionals who can help you. They can provide counseling and medication, if needed, as well as other resources to help you cope. They can help you learn to better handle stress and life problems.

You matter! Make your mental health a priority. When you do, you will experience deep personal growth and be able to better help others. You can learn to become stronger so that you can bounce back from hard things.

This chapter covers the following topics:

- Trauma
- Bouncing Back
- Caring for Your Mental Health
- Attitudes About Mental Health
- Common Mental Health Difficulties

# Trauma

Just about everyone who has been to prison has experienced trauma. Trauma is the emotional response you have during a stressful and possibly life-changing event. It can also be the result of toxic stress that builds up over time. Trauma is more common than people think, and its effects can be very serious. Traumatic events that you had as a child can have effects throughout your life.

People in prison, especially women, are more likely to have experienced trauma. There are strong connections between trauma, poor mental health, and incarceration.

*Trauma is something that all of us go through. You have to get to the point that you realize that what you've been going through is trauma. Nothing you went through is normal. It's not normal to be secluded. Even before prison, we were on the streets, experiencing trauma and violence to the point that it became a natural thing. We became desensitized to those things. We didn't think, 'Oh wow, this is abnormal.'*

**—Anonymous**

*The residue of prison stays with you. Keys rattling means it's a guard coming. You wake up with a heightened sense of alertness. You are late and you worry you have missed your chance. You can't calm down. You have a pattern of sleeplessness. You are easily annoyed. Tense situations escalate into violence.*

**—Kilroy**

Trauma can come from lots of things, such as:
- Physical, sexual, or emotional abuse
- Neglect
- Witnessing violence
- Having a loved one with substance use or mental health difficulties
- Parent separation or divorce
- Poverty
- Being incarcerated or having a family member who is incarcerated
- Living in an unsafe neighborhood

**Where to get help.** If you have experienced trauma, you may benefit from treatment or counseling. Counselors can help you understand the effects of trauma on your wellbeing, your emotions, and your behaviors.

Treatment for trauma can provide you with skills to better understand what happened to you. You can learn to cope with the emotions and memories connected to these experiences. The goal is to help you reach a healthier new understanding of what took place in your life.

Here are a few places you can go for help:
- Go to this directory to find a mental health provider: tinyurl.com/samhsa2023 . When calling to set up an appointment, ask if they provide trauma-focused treatment.
- Contact your state's Department of Human Services.
- Your primary care provider (sometimes called your PCP) may be able to connect you to a mental health consultant located in your clinic, so ask if one is available.
- Many reentry programs provide trauma-informed care (see the resource directory on p. 135). Ask what services they provide.

# Bouncing Back

When you face trauma or stress and overcome it, you can strengthen your ability to bounce back from hard things. Being able to bounce back instead of getting stuck is called resilience.

Being resilient does not mean that stress is not hard for you. It means you have taught yourself to better cope with hard things. Resilience can be learned. It is not a trait that only some people have. It is like a muscle that everyone has the ability to strengthen. It takes time and work, but it can be done. There is hope!

If you feel stuck or are not making progress, seek help from a mental health professional. Seeking help is an important part of building resilience.

According to the American Psychological Association, there are four main areas of resilience. You can work to develop each area:

1. **Build connections**

   Connect with people you trust and who understand you. Remind yourself that you are not alone. If you have experienced trauma, it is common to want to isolate yourself. Fight that urge. Find a group to join and get active in the community.

2. **Foster wellness**

   *Take care of your body.* Your body needs good food, sleep, water, and exercise to fight off stress. When you take care of your body, you will feel better. There is a big connection between your physical and mental health.

   *Practice mindfulness.* Mindfulness is being in the present moment without judgment. It can be practiced in many different ways. See our mindfulness chapter to learn more about (on p. 126).

   *Avoid negative outlets.* When things are stressful it is tempting to want to turn to drugs, alcohol, or other negative ways of coping. This is like putting a bandaid on a large wound. Instead, try to focus on healthy things you can give your body to help you cope.

Mapping Your Future, National Edition

*Having a support group provides you with a reminder that there are other ways to cope.*

**—Kilroy**

*In prison I had ways to cope with trauma. I would exercise, draw. This allowed me to escape that mental state for a little while.*

**—Anonymous**

3. **Find purpose**

    *Help others.* Find meaning and purpose by helping others. Get involved with a community organization or help a friend who is struggling.

    *Be proactive.* Ask yourself, "What can I do about this problem?" Set achievable goals and break them down into smaller steps. Start working on these steps.

    *Look for opportunities for self-discovery.* Self-awareness can help you grow. Think about how you have grown because of a struggle, like being locked up. How have you become a better person? You may find that it helps you increase self-worth and appreciate your path in life.

4. **Embrace healthy thoughts**

    *Keep things in perspective.* You cannot always control events in your life. But you can control how you make sense of things and respond to them. How you think about your situation impacts how you feel, so try not to dwell on those negative thoughts.

    *Accept change.* Being able to accept change is a part of life. Everything changes, and some changes may get in the way of your goals. Focus instead on the things that are in your power to change and control. As the saying goes, "Grant me the serenity to accept what I cannot change, the courage to change what I can, and the wisdom to know the difference."

    *Maintain a hopeful outlook.* It is not realistic to be positive all the time. Allow yourself to feel upset for a little bit, but then focus on what gives you hope. What do you want and how can you make that happen?

    *Learn from your past.* Look back at what has helped you through hard times. Remind yourself of where you found strength before. What have you learned about yourself from your past experiences?

*Advice for socializing outside? Learning coping skills and anger management. Being less abrasive and open-minded.*

**—Earl W.**

# Reflect

1. What has helped you "bounce back" from hard things in the past?

2. What are some things you would like to try to strengthen your resilience muscles?

# Caring for Your Mental Health

## Seeking Treatment for Your Mental Health

**Everyone can benefit from mental health support during reentry.** Reentry is stressful. Even if you do not have mental health difficulties, you may benefit from talking to someone to help you adjust.

It is a good idea to schedule an appointment with a mental health provider before your release. Many community mental health centers have long waiting lists, so set up an appointment ahead of time. This will help you get the support you need when things are tough.

There are several different options for care, depending on your needs.

## Crisis Care

Are you in a crisis? Are you worried about hurting yourself or others? Do you have suicidal thoughts? Are you seeing and hearing things that aren't there? Are your symptoms getting in the way of everyday activities?

If so, find help right away. Here are a few places you can turn to:

- **National Suicide and Crisis Lifeline:** Call 988 or go to 988lifeline.org to get help and chat with someone.
- **National Online Chat:** Visit suicidepreventionlifeline.org/chat. The Lifeline Chat is open 24/7.
- **Crisis Text Line:** Text "HELLO" to 741741. This service is also available 24/7.

If you or someone you know is in immediate danger

- **call 911** and ask for a C.I.T. (Crisis Intervention Trained) officer, or
- **go to the nearest emergency room.**

If you are in crisis, you may be given an emergency evaluation to see if you need to be hospitalized. Hospital treatments during a crisis are very brief. They are meant to keep you safe and get you stable. You'll get connected to on-going treatment options when you leave the hospital.

After your crisis has passed, be sure to follow up with a mental health professional in your community.

## Non-Crisis Care

If you need help but it's not an emergency, find a community provider for treatment. When you call, ask for a mental health assessment or intake with a therapist or counselor, or, for medication, with a psychiatrist.

These resources will help you find a community provider near you:

- **National Directory of Mental Health Treatment Facilities:** Find this nationwide directory of mental health service providers at tinyurl.com/samhsa2023 .
- **Your primary care provider:** Ask your primary care provider if they can connect you to a local mental health consultant.
- **Treatment Referral Helpline:** Call the Substance Abuse and Mental Health Services Administration at (800) 662-4357.
- **Department of Health and Human Services Treatment Locator:** Use this online service to find local help: findtreatment.gov .

## Types of Treatment

There are different mental health professionals who can make a diagnosis and provide treatment.

- **Counselors, Social Workers, and Family Therapists** offer assessment, diagnosis, and treatment of mental health difficulties through counseling.
- **Clinical Psychologists** diagnose and treat mental health difficulties through counseling. They also can also offer testing of behaviors, emotions, and thoughts. This testing can be helpful for making a diagnosis.
- **Psychiatrists** also assess, diagnose, and treat mental health difficulties, but they take a medical approach and can prescribe medications.

Often, it's helpful to combine different types of treatment, like therapy and medication.

**The most important part of treatment is not the type of treatment you choose but the relationship you have with your mental health provider.** Most mental health professionals have different specialties. If you are able to, find someone who has training and experience working with the problems you face.

Make sure that you feel safe and connected to your provider so that you can benefit from treatment. If you do not feel safe and connected, seek alternative care.

**Individual therapy or counseling.** Counseling involves working one-on-one with a mental health professional. This kind of therapy can help you heal, grow, and move toward a more productive and healthier life. A therapist will help you learn to live your best life by introducing you to tools that will help you cope with changes to your mental health.

**Group therapy or counseling.** This is similar to individual treatment, but you will do therapy with other people. These are not self-help groups. A mental health professional will lead the group. You will likely attend weekly sessions. The power of group treatment comes from the group members. It can be helpful to have a support network of others who have similar challenges. Many groups target a specific problem, but some may be more general.

*I benefited a lot from [my support group]. Everybody in those meetings had a similar experience. We are at a place now where we can reflect on some of the things we went through. Maturity comes with age. They have been part of my unofficial therapy.*

**—Anonymous**

**Family therapy or counseling.** The goal of family therapy is to improve relationships and resolve conflicts. It can include your romantic partner, children, and other family members. It is often used with other types of treatments.

*Many conflicts arise because your family has no idea what you've gone through in prison. Or they don't understand your diagnosis. Families need a guide for what it's like for those of us who have been through prison, who have experienced trauma.*

**—Kilroy**

**Medication.** Just as medication can treat heart disease and diabetes, medication can treat mental health difficulties. Medications are not always needed, but most people with moderate to severe mental health difficulties benefit from medication.

Bipolar disorder and schizophrenia symptoms cannot be managed without the help of medication. If you have been diagnosed with one of these disorders, make sure you take your medication every day. Don't skip doses. If you have severe anxiety or depression, you will also likely benefit from medication. Taking medication can help relieve symptoms so that you feel better. Combined with counseling, medication can help you lead a healthier and more productive life.

Medications are prescribed by a psychiatrist or psychiatric nurse practitioner after a brief evaluation. Your psychiatrist will monitor your medications and side effects. It takes time for your body to adjust to medications. It also takes time for your provider to find what works best for you. Many medications have side effects, especially when you first take them. Don't give up if the first medication isn't for you. It may take a couple of tries to find the right medicine and dosage.

**Warning: Don't quit taking medication once you start feeling better.** Feeling good may be a sign that the medication is working, not that you don't need it anymore! Always consult with a psychiatric practitioner before stopping your medications. Stopping medications all at once can be very dangerous. Your psychiatrist can help you stop gradually and safely.

**Paying for Treatment.** Medicaid will cover mental health treatment. If you need to apply for Medicaid, the Health chapter tells you how (see p. 62). Not all mental health treatment programs accept Medicaid. Make sure to ask if the program accepts Medicaid when you call to make your first appointment. If you do not have insurance, some programs will also offer services on a "sliding fee scale." This lets you pay what you can afford.

Most programs that accept Medicaid have long waiting lists, so plan ahead. If possible, make your appointments before your release.

If you are enrolling in private insurance, make sure to select a plan that includes mental health treatment. When you make an appointment, ask if they accept your insurance. You may be able to see a mental health professional in private practice. This may decrease your waiting time for an appointment.

# Attitudes About Mental Health

Some people feel embarrassed or ashamed of having mental health difficulties. These attitudes may have come from your family, your community, or from the media. These attitudes can make it hard for you to get better.

Everyone has a role in the fight against these negative attitudes! The National Alliance on Mental Illness (NAMI) offers some suggestions about what you can do to help choose empowerment over shame:

- Think of physical and mental illness in similar ways. Lots of people have mental health difficulties, just as lots of people have physical health difficulties, like diabetes and heart disease. Getting treatment is a positive thing.
- Talk openly about mental health. Share your experience with people you trust.
- Educate yourself and others. Respond to negative comments by sharing facts and experiences.
- Be conscious of language. Remind people that words matter. Try to avoid using words like "crazy" or "insane" when what you mean is that something is frustrating or poorly thought out. This misuse can cause shame and hurt.
- Show compassion for those with mental health difficulties, including yourself.
- Be honest about treatment. Getting mental health treatment is normal, just like other healthcare treatment.

*In prison, people tend to mock those who go through a mental health episode. Everyone knows who's taking pills. You condition yourself to not talk. You don't want to express your feelings or admit something is wrong.*

**—Kilroy**

*When I first met with the group, guys would just sit there. They wouldn't open up. So I opened myself up. I'd tell them, this is what's been bothering me. Break the ice. Then someone else would talk about their experience.*

**—Kilroy**

*It's all right to show your emotions. It's a natural thing to vent, to cry.*

**—Anonymous**

Mapping Your Future, National Edition

 # Reflect

1. What negative attitudes do you have about working on your own mental health?

2. Where do these negative attitudes come from? Try to be specific as you think about this question.

3. What are some things you can do to challenge these negative attitudes?

..........................................................................................

# Common Mental Health Difficulties

Several mental health difficulties are common in people who spend time in prison. We describe them here so that you can know what they look like, if you struggle with them, and when you may need to get help.

**Major depressive disorder.** Everyone feels sad once in a while, but not everyone feels depressed. Symptoms include:

- Feeling sad or uninterested in things most of the time
- Changes in eating and sleeping habits
- Feeling low energy and having a hard time focusing
- Feeling tearful, empty, hopeless, or angry and irritable
- Feeling miserable but not understanding why
- Some people also have chronic pain or digestive issues

Do these symptoms last for at least two weeks? Do they get in the way of your everyday life? You may be depressed, even if you're only having some of these symptoms. Counseling and/or medicine can help.

If you are **severely depressed**, you may also have thoughts of wanting to hurt yourself or die. Severe depression may also cause you to hear or see things that are not there. If you have these severe symptoms, go to the nearest emergency room right away or call the National Suicide and Crisis Lifeline at 988.

**Bipolar disorder.** Most people have changes in mood at times. If you're stressed, you might feel angry or scared. If you lost someone you love, you might feel sad. Hormone changes can also affect moods.

But if you have intense mood swings that last for several days, you may have bipolar disorder. People with bipolar disorder have extreme shifts in mood, energy, and ability to function. These mood shifts include episodes of depression (see above) and mania. Signs of mania are:

- Increased self-esteem, like you are on top of the world
- Less need for sleep
- Talking a lot and often fast
- Having so many thoughts that you cannot keep up with them
- Being distracted easily
- Feeling restless, pacing, bouncing your legs
- Doing things that are risky and can cause harm, like spending too much money, having unprotected sex with various partners, or using drugs or alcohol

For some people, manic and depressive episodes can be extreme. Sometimes symptoms include seeing and hearing things that are not there. If your symptoms are severe, get help right away. Managing bipolar disorder requires help from medicine and counseling.

If you think this might sound like something you struggle with, keep a record of your mood changes.

This will help you to know if you need to seek help. It may also help your healthcare provider to make a diagnosis and treatment plan.

**Generalized anxiety disorder.** Feeling anxious or stressed once in a while is a normal part of life. If your anxiety feels out of control, you might have an anxiety disorder. Generalized anxiety disorder is when you worry a lot and are nervous about everyday things, even things that you have no control over, for little or no reason. You might feel like something really bad is going to happen. Anxiety leaves you feeling restless, tired, irritable, and tense. It can impact your ability to focus and sleep.

If these problems do not go away and begin to impact your relationships and responsibilities, get help. Counseling can help. Medication can help when symptoms are severe.

**Schizophrenia.** Some people can have a distorted sense of reality. In some cases, this is known as schizophrenia. It is a severe mental health condition that requires medication. Counseling (in addition to medicine) can help you build life skills to cope. Schizophrenia involves a range of problems with thinking, behavior, and emotions. Signs of schizophrenia can vary, but it usually involves:

- Problems with thinking (having a hard time organizing your thoughts, forgetting things, not being able to focus, struggling to make decisions)
- Delusions (false beliefs that are not based in reality)
- Hallucinations (seeing or hearing things that aren't really there)
- Disorganized speech (not being able to put words or sentences together)
- Lacking common skills, like the ability to express emotion, be part of activities, and engage with others

These symptoms can have a big impact on your life. If you think you may be experiencing these symptoms, seek help as soon as you can.

**Post-traumatic stress disorder (PTSD).** Some traumatic events are so shocking, damaging, or dangerous that they can change the way we think and feel long after the event has passed. It's natural to feel scared, nervous, or depressed after something bad has happened. If these feelings last for over a month, you may have post-traumatic stress disorder (PTSD).

**Common symptoms of PTSD include:**
- Having nightmares or flashbacks
- Avoiding people or situations that remind you of the event
- Feeling on edge and anxious a lot of the time
- Feeling depressed
- Trouble remembering things
- Feeling emotionally detached

Medications and counseling can be useful in working through these symptoms.

**Personality disorders.** Your personality is who you are: the thoughts, patterns, feelings, and behaviors that define you. Sometimes people can develop personality disorders. These are patterns and traits that are harmful to the person experiencing them and to others. For people in prison, the two most common personality disorders are borderline personality disorder and antisocial personality disorder.

- People with **borderline personality disorder** have unstable moods, behavior, and relationships. They often feel emotionally unstable, worthless, insecure, or impulsive. These feelings or behaviors hurt their relationships.
- People with **antisocial personality disorder** act in ways that show a lack of care about other people. For example, they may lie, break laws, or act impulsively. Often, they do not care about their own safety or the safety of others.

Since personality traits are pretty stable over our lifetime, these disorders can be hard to treat. Despite that, treatment is possible. It often includes long-term therapy. Medications do not tend to work well for these disorders.

**Multiple mental health challenges.** Many people who are in prison have more than one mental health disorder. People who have depression are more likely to have anxiety, too. Many people who have a mental health disorder also have a substance use problem. Some people have a mental health disorder, a personality disorder, and a substance use disorder.

If you think you might be struggling with one—or more—of these difficulties, talk to a healthcare professional. Tell them everything. If you tell them about one problem but not another, you may find it difficult to fully recover.

# Substance Use

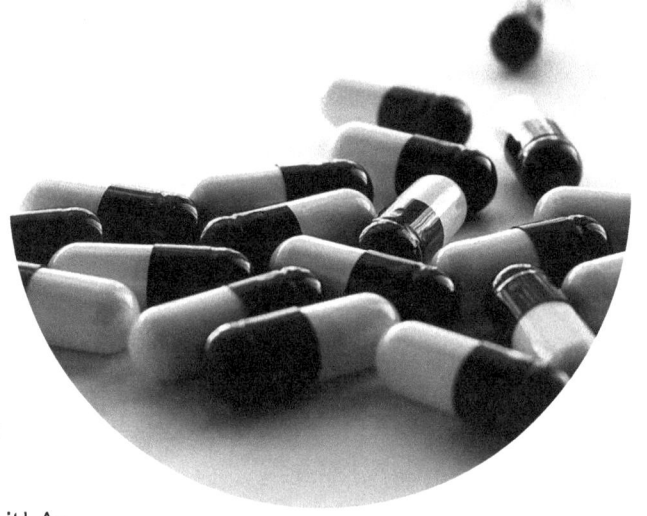

Do you have difficulty controlling your use of alcohol, illegal drugs, or medications? If so, this is one of the most important chapters you will read. As you know, drug and alcohol problems can make it much harder to get a job, form healthy relationships, find housing, and stay out of prison.

We urge you to get help. Your reentry success depends upon it! As you begin to recover, your mind will become clearer and you will be better able to rebuild your life.

For many, prison is a time to get clean from drugs or alcohol. But just because you were clean in prison doesn't mean that you are fully recovered. Many people find that problems with drugs or alcohol return when they are released.

Reentry can be a time of stress, anxiety, and fear. You're trying to rebuild your life while also dealing with the trauma of being locked up for years. Perhaps you have used drugs and alcohol to cope with difficult feelings in the past. Recognize that this puts you at greater risk of relapse.

There is hope. Know that many people recover, and you can too. We honor your efforts. Recovery isn't easy, and you may have setbacks. We believe in YOU and your ability to recover.

This chapter covers the following topics:
- Where to Get Help
- Safer Drug Use
- Treatment Programs
- Finding a Peer Support Group
- The Road to Recovery
- New Cannabis Laws

*What ends up happening is you get out and you realize your issues don't end. Now you have to deal with other issues. You get hit with all this stuff. You start to get into bad habits again, revert to old coping mechanisms. You have alcohol available, you have drugs. The bottle becomes more available than the gym.*

**—Anonymous**

# Where to Get Help

Let's be honest. The first few days, weeks, and months after release are really challenging. This is why it's a good idea to make plans to get help before you are released.

It's best if you can set up a time to meet with a treatment provider within two to three days of release. Join a support group like Alcoholics Anonymous right away, or make an appointment to see a counselor. Don't wait to get help.

Here are a few places you can start:
- **National Helpline:** Call (800) 662-4357 or visit their website to find help near you: findtreatment.samhsa.gov .
- **National sober house directory:** soberhousedirectory.com .
- **Peer support groups:** Find an Alcoholics Anonymous support group by calling (855) 977-9213 or going to aa.org. Find a Narcotics Anonymous support group by calling (818) 773-9999 or going to na.org.

For more details and information on finding non-religious support groups, see the section of this chapter titled "Finding a Peer Support Group" (below).

☆ **If you have overdosed and need immediate help, call 911.**

# Safer Drug Use

Many substance use treatment programs focus on getting clean or sobering up. There are many reasons you may want to do this. You may need to pass drug tests as a condition of your parole. Many jobs require drug testing.

Some people find that quitting completely is the only thing that works for them. If they start drinking a little, this quickly turns back into drinking a lot. Groups like Alcoholics Anonymous encourage quitting completely and provide peer support to reach this goal.

Quitting isn't easy. Many people can quit for a while, but then return to occasional drug use. If this is your experience, there are things you can do to **reduce the harm** of drug use in your life. There are ways to manage your drug use so that it doesn't take over your life. Moderating your use of drugs or alcohol is a worthy goal. Work with a counselor or program that offers substance use management.

 **Warning:** Did you know that people who have recently returned from prison are at greater risk for overdose? If you stopped using drugs or alcohol while in prison, you may have a reduced tolerance for these drugs. This means that your body can't handle the same amount of drugs that you took before. This can lead to overdose or even death.

Here are a few safety tips:
- Learn how to inject safely and care for your veins to avoid getting HIV or another disease: anypositivechange.org/better-vein-care .
- Find out if there are organizations in your area that offer safer injecting equipment.
- Learn the signs of overdose and how to respond. Teach your friends and family to recognize these signs, too. Check for organizations in your area that can provide naloxone (commonly called Narcan), a drug that reverses opiate overdose.

### Signs of an Overdose:
- Unresponsive or unconscious
- Slow or stopped breathing
- Snoring or gurgling sounds
- Cold, clammy skin
- Blue lips, discolored fingernails

**What to do:** Try to wake the person. Call 911 if you can't. Start CPR if their breathing is slow or they have stopped breathing. Provide naloxone (Narcan) if available.

 # Reflect

Whether your goal is safer drug use or quitting entirely, take time to reflect on your drug or alcohol use. Here are a few things to reflect on, either alone or with a counselor:

1. Where do you use and when? Can you find ways to separate drug use from driving or working tasks?

2. Who do you use with? How are your relationships helping or hurting your recovery? How can you navigate these relationships to quit or be safer?

3. What are your habits or personal rituals around drug use? Can you modify those rituals so that you use less or use in safer ways?

4. Think about your attitudes and emotions about drug use, such as shame and guilt. How are these emotions getting in the way of your recovery?

5. What stresses or emotions trigger your use? What are some more helpful ways to deal with difficult emotions?

*What I felt was most difficult when I first got out is figuring out how to relate to other people. You have both the lack of 'normal' experiences that most people have as late-teenagers and young adults. Plus you have the negative effects of long-term imprisonment.*

**—Greg A.**

# Treatment Programs

There are many kinds of treatment programs. There are options for inpatient and outpatient care to help you with substance use. An inpatient program means that you live in a facility with 24/7 care and support, such as a rehab center or recovery home. An outpatient program means that you go to a facility to receive care during the day, but you still live at home. There are intensive outpatient programs where you go frequently during the week. There are also peer support groups and therapy sessions that meet less frequently. Both inpatient and outpatient treatment is helpful. The type of care you pick depends on your situation. For help deciding what is right for you, visit: startyourrecovery.org/treatment/rehab-centers/outpatient-vs-inpatient . If you have severe difficulties with substance use, at least three months of intensive treatment is recommended. After that, follow-up support can be helpful for months and even years.

Some treatments will focus on helping you to manage the stress and triggers that have led you to use in the past. Some treatments include doctors who can prescribe medications (such as methadone, buprenorphine, and naltrexone) to help you overcome an addiction. All good treatment programs should:

- **Empower you.** It should build upon your strengths. It shouldn't shame you. It should help you take an active role in your recovery.
- **Provide mental health treatment.** Many people who have substance use disorders also struggle with mental health. It is essential to treat both mental health and substance use issues together.
- **Address past trauma.** Many people use drugs to cope with past trauma. A good treatment program will help you develop effective coping strategies and recover from the effects of trauma and violence.
- **Provide support services.** Recovery is about more than getting clean. Good treatment programs offer services to help you rebuild your life. They may help you find employment and safe housing.

**Are you pregnant? Do you have children you are caring for?** For the sake of you and your children, reach out and get help. Many women are afraid their children will be taken away if their substance use becomes known. But continuing to use drugs or alcohol also puts you and your children at great risk.

As you are surely aware, society is not kind to mothers with substance use problems. You have likely sensed how harshly people judge you. You may have intense feelings of guilt and shame. We recommend that you seek out a treatment program that can help with the unique challenges women and mothers face.

Always let your doctor know if you are pregnant or think you may be pregnant before starting a medical treatment for substance use. Some medications are not safe to take while pregnant or nursing.

**Paying for Treatment.** Medicaid covers the cost of many substance use treatment services, such as counseling, therapy, medication management, social work services, and peer support. Our Health chapter explains how to apply for Medicaid (see p. 62). Not all treatment programs accept Medicaid. Before starting services, ask if they accept Medicaid.

If you are enrolling in a private insurance plan, choose a plan that covers substance use treatment. When making an appointment with a service provider or clinic, check that they accept your insurance.

Even if you do not yet have insurance, there are affordable clinics and programs that you can go to for help. Look for "sliding scale" services where you pay only what you can afford.

 # Finding a Peer Support Group

If you are struggling with drug or alcohol use, join a support group to get help and encouragement from others. These groups are usually free.

☆ *Becoming Ms. Burton: From Prison to Recovery to Leading the Fight for Incarcerated Women* is the inspiring autobiography written by the civil and human rights activist Susan Burton. She struggled with addiction and was incarcerated many times before starting her own nonprofit organization devoted to helping formerly incarcerated people.

In *Becoming Ms. Burton*, Susan Burton describes how her first Alcoholics Anonymous group meeting gave her hope:

> *People stood up and shared their stories.... I rose, took a deep breath. "Look what drugs and alcohol have done to me," I said, my voice quivering. My hands were shaking so much the styrofoam cup of coffee I held was wasting on me. But no one seemed to judge my piteous condition. The immediate compassion, the empathy, the love that rolled off these strangers was enough to put a sizable dent in my pain, my shame, my guilt, and all that sorrow. In that room, I found hope.*

Alcoholics Anonymous (AA) and Narcotics Anonymous (NA) are the largest peer recovery organizations and have chapters throughout the country. Visit aa.org or na.org to find a meeting or online group. AA and NA use a religious approach, though they are not tied to a specific religion. Their 12-step process begins by asking members to admit that they no longer have control over their drug or alcohol use. Members are asked to turn themselves over to a higher power to find the strength to change.

There are non-religious support group options, too. These options focus on helping people find motivation within themselves. Here are a few popular options, with in person and online meetings throughout the US:

- **Self-Management and Recovery Training (SMART)** peer support groups help participants resolve problems with any addiction. Go to smartrecovery.org or call (440) 951-5357 to find a meeting or online community.
- **Women for Sobriety** is a peer-support program for women overcoming substance use disorders. Go to womenforsobriety.org or call (215) 536-8026 to find an in-person or online meeting.
- **Secular Organizations for Sobriety** is a network of peer groups to help people maintain sobriety/abstinence from alcohol and drug addictions, food addiction, and more. Go to sossobriety.org or call (314) 353-3532 to find a meeting.
- **LifeRing Secular Recovery** is an organization of people who share practical experiences and sobriety support. They focus on empowering you to overcome your addiction. Go to lifering.org or call (800) 811-4142 to find a meeting.

Ask your primary care provider for recommendations. Many community centers and churches also sponsor support groups or can direct you to others.

Approach your first meeting with an open mind and try to find out all you can. You may need to attend several meetings before you feel things are "clicking." If you don't feel you have found your group, keep trying. Chapters can be very different and members come and go. Look for:

- Regularly scheduled meetings
- Warmth and friendliness
- Some focus and structure to meetings
- Some time to mingle informally

 ## Reflect

1. What treatments (medication, therapy, peer support groups) have you tried in the past?

2. How have these treatments helped you? What worked and what didn't work?

3. What kinds of treatment would you like to try?

4. Where can you go for help?

 ## The Road to Recovery

The road to recovery can be a long one. Don't be too discouraged if you relapse. A relapse doesn't always mean that the treatment isn't working. Give it another chance. Recognize that if you stopped using once, you can again. You have developed skills that will help you next time. Ask if there is a different treatment that may work better for you. Sometimes multiple periods of treatment are needed.

Recovery isn't just about the need to stop using. It's about the need for change. It's about improving your overall health and wellness. It's about living up to your full potential. The Substance Abuse and Mental Health Services Administration (SAMHSA) lists four main aspects of recovery:

1. **Health:** Overcome or manage one's disease or symptoms
2. **Home:** Find a stable and safe place to live
3. **Purpose:** Take part in meaningful daily activities (job, school, family caretaking, etc.)
4. **Community:** Build relationships and social networks that provide support, friendship, love, and hope

 ## Reflect

1. What does recovery look like to you?

2. Where are you on your road toward recovery?

3. What are some good short term goals you can work towards?

*Mapping Your Future, National Edition*

# New Cannabis Laws

The U.S. has a long history of punishing people, especially people of color, for minor drug offenses, such as possession of marijuana. Too often, people with substance use issues are sent to prison instead of getting the treatment and support they need. The war on drugs has greatly increased the number of people of color locked up in the US.

You have likely heard that marijuana is now fully legal in some states. Other states only legalized CBD or medical-use marijuana. With these changes, you may be interested in getting a pardon or sealing your record for a marijuana-related offense. See the table below to find your state's policy as of January 2024.

| Marijuana is legalized* | Marijuana has a mixed legalization status | Marijuana is fully illegal |
|---|---|---|
| Alaska, Arizona, California, Colorado, Connecticut, Delaware, Illinois, Maine, Maryland, Massachusetts, Michigan, Minnesota, Missouri, Montana, Nevada, New Jersey, New Mexico, New York, Ohio, Oregon, Rhode Island, Vermont, Virginia, Washington | Alabama, Arkansas, Florida, Georgia, Hawaii, Indiana, Iowa, Kentucky, Louisiana, Mississippi, Nebraska, New Hampshire, North Carolina, North Dakota, Oklahoma, Pennsylvania, South Dakota, Tennessee, Texas, Utah, West Virginia, Wisconsin | Idaho, Kansas, South Carolina, Wyoming |

*In states where marijuana has been legalized, adults over the age of 21 have the right to buy a state-determined amount of marijuana from a licensed dispensary. The amount will vary depending on where you are, and there may be other limitations around distribution or based on product type. Make sure to check your state-specific laws and limitations here: norml.org/laws .

 **Warning:** Make sure to check with your parole officer about marijuana possession, usage, or distribution, even if marijuana has been legalized in your state.

# Transportation

How are you going to get around? Transportation is important for your job, for spending time with friends and family, and for living a meaningful life. Unfortunately, it can cost a lot.

If you return to a large city, you'll have many transportation options. In small towns, your choices might be more limited. Below we discuss the options and a few practical details.

This chapter covers:
- Transportation Options (buses, trains, taxis, bikes, cars, and more)
- Buying a Car
- Driving Legally

 # Transportation Options

## Buses and Metro

You can save money with public transportation. In most cities, if you use the bus or metro often, you can buy a month- or year-long pass. This will make the cost of each ride cheaper. Students, older people, veterans, or people with disabilities can get discounts. Here are a few ways to get started:

- Search for "public transportation" with the name of your city. Many systems have online route maps and offer discounts.
- Visit the website www.google.com/maps or open a map app on your phone. Enter your starting point and you'd like to end up. The website or app will give step-by-step instructions for public transportation.

## Trains and Long-Distance Buses

Here are a few good options for longer trips:

- Amtrak (trains) is a good way to travel long distances. It has service to many places around the country. Go to amtrak.com for more information.
- Greyhound, BoltBus, and MegaBus are a few long-distance bus companies. Bus tickets can be purchased online or in person.

It is always a good idea to compare prices between trains, planes, and buses, as well as between bus companies.

## Ride-hailing Apps and Taxis

If you have a smartphone and a credit or debit card, you can get a ride-hailing or "rideshare" app like Uber or Lyft. These apps allow you to hail your own ride or share a ride with someone else. They can take you on short trips in your city. These services work like taxis, but the drivers use their own cars. Before you ride, read these tips on how to be safe at uber.com/us/en/ride/safety/tips . Prices can vary widely between apps and at different times of day.

You can still use taxis in all major cities. They usually cost more than ride-hailing apps.

## Biking

Biking is a good way to save money and get exercise. In some cities you can rent bikes, but this often requires using a smartphone app or possibly a website. You can also look for stores that sell used bikes (many bike stores do, even if they don't advertise it). If you bike, make sure you know the rules of the road. Usually, bicycles follow the same rules as cars. They have to stop at stop signs and stop lights. You must use hand signals to turn or switch lanes. And you must yield to pedestrians. Wear a helmet to avoid head injuries. For more information on safe riding, visit bikepgh.org/ride-safe or bicyclesafe.com .

Most map apps, like Google Maps will provide bike routes as well. Just type in your destination and hit the bike icon to get directions for how to travel by bike.

*Mapping Your Future, National Edition*

## Carpool, Rideshare, and Carshare Programs

Another option for saving money is to carpool. You can look up carpool programs online to carpool with strangers. Or you can ask someone you know if you can carpool and share the cost of gas.

If you don't need a car very often, join a carsharing program like Zipcar. Zipcar lets you reserve a car when you need it. You won't have to pay for insurance, repairs, or any of the things that make owning a car so expensive.

# Buying a Car

If you do buy a car, make sure to consider the bills you will need to pay every month. The down payment is just the beginning. A few tips:

1. **Budget.** If you are taking out a loan to buy a car, make a budget. Decide how much you can spend on monthly payments. See the "Finances, Credit, and Taxes" chapter (on p. 96) for more information on buying with credit and budgeting.
2. **Research.** Do some research on the types of cars that will meet your needs. Think about what will be safe and reliable. Edmunds.com and Consumerreports.org are great places to start. You can look at how much the cars are worth by going to Kelley's Blue Book (kbb.com).
3. **Buy from a place you can trust.** Don't go to car dealerships that say they sell to people with bad credit. Be suspicious of companies or people who push you into buying a vehicle before you are ready. Buying directly from a person can be cheaper, but it is also riskier than buying from a trustworthy dealer.
4. **Check out the history.** Once you've found a car you like, ask the dealer if you can see its history report. Ask for the Vehicle Identification Number (VIN). You can check a car's history online at websites like autotrader.com .
5. **Mechanic.** If you are buying from a dealer, make sure that the car passes a mechanical evaluation. If you are buying from a person, ask a mechanic to look at it before you buy it.
6. **Negotiate the price.** Check prices on cars like the one you want to buy, and go to more than one place to compare cars. This can help you negotiate a good deal.
7. **Read the fine print.** Understand the contract before you sign anything. Remember, what counts is what is in the contract, not what the salesperson promised. Make sure that you fill out all of the paperwork you need, especially if you are buying from an individual owner.
8. **Title and registration.** Make sure to get the title and registration before you give them any money.

# Driving Legally

## Car Insurance

In many states, you must have car insurance and a driver's license (see the Getting Your ID chapter on p. 30) to drive. If you are pulled over and you don't have insurance, you may have to pay a fine. You can also get charged, which in some states may be a violation of parole.

When you have car insurance, you pay a monthly fee (sometimes called a "premium"), and then the insurance covers some of the costs if you get in an accident. Check to see what kind of insurance your state requires. It may require one or both of the following:

- **Liability insurance:** This covers the costs if you cause an accident.
- **Uninsured and underinsured motorist insurance:** This covers costs for you and your passengers if you get in an accident with someone who doesn't have insurance, or not enough insurance.

Some insurance plans cover most or all the costs if you are in an accident. Some do not. Some have different costs if you caused the accident or if someone else did. If you get in an accident, your monthly payments may increase.

Buying car insurance can be confusing. Here are a few tips:

- Talk to an agent by phone or in person. Don't sign up online.
- Find out what the maximum amount of coverage is for the plan. This is the amount they will pay if you hit a car. You would have to pay anything above this amount.
- Your state's DMV website may provide more information on insurance and prices.

## Car Registration

In many states you have to register your car. You will have to renew this registration every year, for a fee. If you don't register your car or renew it, you can get a big ticket. You may be able to register your car online, or you may have to go to your local DMV. Check their website to find out what you need to bring.

## Car Inspection

Your car also may need to get inspected for emissions and safety. If you get your car inspected and it does not pass, you will need to fix its problems before getting it inspected again. Not all cars need to be inspected in all states. To find out if your car needs inspections, check with your Secretary of State. Some states allow you to check online by typing in your vehicle VIN (Vehicle Identification Number).

## Rules of the Road

Be safe when you drive. We care about you! Don't drink alcohol before driving. Don't text or use your phone while driving. Pull over to make a call. Wear your seatbelt; it reduces your chance of death in the event of a serious accident by 50 percent!

 **Reflect**

1. What are my transportation needs? What are my transportation options?

2. What transportation options are new to me, and how can I learn more about these options?

3. What do I need to do to prepare to get a car? What will I need to do after my purchase?

# Technology

Technology has changed a lot in the last few years. If you have been inside a long time, you might feel stressed by all the new technology. Don't worry! You'll be able to figure it out.

You will need phones and computers for a lot of things after you leave prison. You will use them for work, banking, communicating, making appointments, meeting with parole officers, ordering pizza, watching TV shows, paying bills, shopping, applying for jobs, and much more.

Ask your family and friends to help you learn how to use a cell phone, smartphone, or computer. Learning how to use them can be fun. Play around with games, news, and sports apps, or even watch cat videos! Playing can help you learn to use them. Take your time and get used to the technology that you use—soon it will feel like second nature.

This chapter covers the following topics:

- Getting a Phone
- Technology Basics
- Using the Internet
- Email, Passwords, and Security
- Smartphone Apps
- Social Media
- Video Conferencing
- Digital Literacy Resources

 ## Getting a Phone

We recommend getting a phone when you get out. You will need a phone to keep in contact with family, friends, your employer, and your parole officer. There are three types of phones:

- **Landlines or landline phones** are phones connected to people's homes or businesses. They can't move around. Fewer people are using landline phones these days, but they are still one of the cheapest kinds of phone.
- **Basic cell phones** let you call people and send text messages. They are cheaper than smartphones and easy to use.
- **Smartphones** can make calls and send text messages, and you can use them to get on the internet. Smartphones have programs (called "apps") that can do things like play music, give driving directions, check the weather, take pictures, and go on social networks like LinkedIn and Facebook. A smartphone can help you find jobs, look up services, find your way around, and more.

## Lifeline and SafeLink

Do you have Medicaid, SNAP, SSI, or Public Housing Assistance? If you do, you should be able to get a free or discounted phone or internet. SafeLink will provide you with each of these for free:

- Smartphone
- A SIM card. This small card goes into your phone and lets it connect to a mobile network.
- Phone plan. A phone plan lets you text, make calls, and use data (get online information and use websites).

Lifeline is a program that works with SafeLink to lower the monthly cost of phone and internet. Lifeline can be used for phone or internet, but not both.

**How to apply.** When you apply for public benefits (such as SNAP or Medicaid; see Resources to Meet Your Basic Needs, p. 32), ask if you can apply for SafeLink and Lifeline as well. If you are eligible, apply for Safelink online at safelinkwireless.com . You can also get help by calling (800) 723-3546. You can apply for Lifeline at lifelinesupport.org . To apply for these services, you will need your contact info, mailing/home address, and Social Security number. You will also need proof that you meet the income requirements. These services are typically limited to one person per household.

## Phone Services and Plans

What if you need to buy your own phone? MetroPCS and Family Mobile (Walmart) are good, cheaper choices. They aren't the best phones, but they won't be too expensive. If you had a cell phone before you were incarcerated, ask your family if they still have the phone. It might still work, and you may want to use it again or change the number. Contact the phone service provider for help with this.

Cell phones come with service plans that you have to pay every month. You have two basic options for service plans:

- **Prepaid phone plans or no-contract plans.** You pay at the start of each month. You can stop your service at the end of each month or switch to a different service.

- **Post-paid phone plan with a contract.** You enter a contract to pay a monthly fee for service. They add up your costs at the end of each billing cycle and charge you. These plans can cost less each month than prepaid phone plans, but make sure you understand the commitments you are agreeing to in your contract.

Phone plans have different options. Generally, the services will cover the following:

- **Talk:** How many minutes you can talk on the phone each month. Many plans these days have unlimited talk time.
- **Text:** How many text messages you can send each month. Many plans these days have unlimited text.
- **Data:** Data lets you use your phone to go on the internet when you don't have access to Wi-Fi (see Technology Basics below). If you only need a phone for calls, you may not need to purchase a data plan. You can use the internet on your phone for free at the library and many other public places and restaurants that offer free Wi-Fi. If you do need data, start with a small amount, like 1 or 2 GB. You can always get more if you need it.

Phone service companies like T-Mobile and MetroPCS have different plans and rates. Some offer deals for sharing a cell phone plan with family members. Think about what you will use your phone for and how much you can afford to spend on it.

## Technology Basics

Here are some technology basics to help you get started.

**Internet:** A network that connects computers and phones all over the world. Through an internet connection, people can share information, access resources, and communicate. Sometimes people call the internet the World Wide Web, or they will say, "you need Web access," which means you need to be able to connect to the internet.

**Online:** When you "are online" or "go online," you are using technology that is connected to the internet. People might say, "Go online to access this resource." This means that you can access the resource over the internet using a computer or smartphone.

**Smartphone:** A phone that does a lot of the things a computer can do. It usually has a touchscreen surface and internet access, and it lets you download apps (short for applications). Apps let smartphones do more things. They help with work, entertainment, money, forecast the weather, and much more. Most people these days have a smartphone.

**Wi-Fi:** To access the internet, you need to be connected to it. One way to do that is through Wi-Fi access. Wi-Fi access allows you to connect to the internet without using wires. You can access Wi-Fi for free at public libraries and some restaurants (McDonalds, Starbucks), or you can buy and install Wi-Fi access for your home.

**Mobile Hotspots:** Some public libraries will have mobile Wi-Fi "hotspots" for you to check out. These are portable devices that you can take anywhere. They will allow you to have internet access outside of the library.

**Data:** Another way to connect to the internet is through a smartphone data plan. Data allows you to connect to the internet on your smartphone if you are in a place that doesn't have Wi-Fi. Data plans can be expensive, and they usually have limits to how much data you can use every month.

**Web browser:** A web browser is a program that allows you to access the internet on your phone or computer. Examples of web browsers are Google Chrome, Firefox, Internet Explorer, and Safari.

**Search engine:** A search engine is what you use when you are trying to find information on the internet. First, you will open a web browser. You should see a bar at the top with a little magnifying glass. If you type a question, the name of a website, or a web address into the bar, a search engine will try to find the information you need. Google, Yahoo, and Bing are examples of search engines.

**Website:** All types of people and organizations have "websites" where you can find information, resources, entertainment, and more. There are millions of websites on the internet of all different types.

**Web address or URL:** This is a website's "address" or location on the internet. Type this address into a web browser's address bar to see the website. We have included many web addresses to websites in this guide and in the directory. Web addresses usually look like this: http://www.examplewebsite.com. When you type in a web address, you can leave out the http:// and www.

*I need assistance with the most basic things. That does make me somewhat defensive, and I'll end up trying to do things on my own and then I crash and burn.*

—**Pablo**

 # Using the Internet

Make sure you have a way to get on the internet when you need to. Until you have your own device, you can borrow one from a friend or family member or use a computer at the public library.

Do you have a smartphone, laptop, or tablet? Free wireless internet is available at the library, as well as many restaurants, coffee shops, hotel lobbies, chain technology stores, and even parks! You may have to ask what the password is before you can log on with your device.

Most people find what they need on the internet by using a search engine. When you start your web browser, the first page it opens will usually have a search box where you can type in what you are looking for.

Here are some tips for good searches:
- Start with the basics. Start with a simple search like "Where's the closest Amtrak?" or "Who won the superbowl?." You can always add more words if you need.
- Search engines understand complete sentences, but they do not require them. Searching for "Who can apply for SNAP benefits in Ohio?" will get similar results to searching for "SNAP eligibility Ohio."
- Don't worry about the little things. Even if you spell things wrong, it should still work.

☆ **Some websites are more reliable than others. Anyone can create a website, and not everything online is true.**

### Getting Help

- Ask a librarian to help you figure out the basics. They are there to help.
- Go to **Northstar** at digitalliteracyassessment.org to test your skills and learn more. You can access classes online or find a Northstar location where you can attend classes. They offer certificates for skills you have mastered.
- GCF Global has a lot of free courses on how to use technology. Type this address in your search engine and click on a topic: edu.gcfglobal.org/en/topics .
- Wikihow also has lots of resources to help you figure out how to use technology. Type "wikihow" in your web browser, and then enter your question in the search box at the top of the page.
- Many community colleges, libraries, and adult basic education programs offer lessons on everything from basic word processing to programming code.

### Affordable Connectivity Program

The FCC (Federal Communications Commission) offers up to $75 per month toward your internet bill and/or a credit of $100 toward the purchase of a computer through their Affordable Connectivity Program. Unfortunately, as of the publication of this guide, the program is on hold due to a lack of funds but may be extended in the future. To learn more, visit affordableconnectivity.gov .

## Email, Passwords, and Security

You will need your own email address. Email is now used more than paper mail. One way to do this is through Gmail, because Gmail accounts are free. Type gmail.com into the web browser and click "Create account."

You will select your own email username. It should be something easy for you to remember, like your own name, or some combination of your name, initials, and numbers. You will probably use your email to apply for jobs, so make sure your email address sounds professional.

Your password should be something easy for you to remember, but hard for other people to figure out.

You will probably use the internet to set up accounts for things like paying bills or accessing files for school or work. Protect your information by keeping your passwords secret and changing them every so often. Don't use the same password for every account you have. If you forget a password, you can usually change it by following instructions on the website. If you had email and other online accounts before you were incarcerated, you may want to reactivate them or close them. Change the passwords to keep everything safe.

☆ If possible, do not put in sensitive personal information (like your Social Security number or credit card information) on a website when you are using a public computer or public Wi-Fi that you can access without a password.

## Smartphone Apps

Most smartphones come with these basic apps:

- Text messaging
- Telephone
- Camera
- Clock
- Web browser (for example, Safari or Chrome)
- Calendar
- Calculator
- Address book (sometimes called "Contacts")
- A map service that can give directions

You can get (or "download") more apps for your phone. They can be found in your phone's "store" (through an app called Apps or Play on most phones). Many useful apps are free. You will need to have either data or a Wi-Fi connection to download apps. If an app costs money, your phone should give

Mapping Your Future, National Edition

you the option to enter your credit or debit card information and will ask you to confirm the purchase before downloading.

Here are some apps you may want to use:
- Facebook Messenger and WhatsApp are text or video messaging apps where you can communicate with family and friends. You can also talk to people in different countries without paying an extra fee.
- Facebook and Instagram let you share and view photos and comments.
- Spotify lets you listen to music.
- Banking apps help you manage your money and pay bills.
- Google Maps, Citymapper, and other transportation apps can help you use public transportation or find your way around.
- Many parole officers use the **BI SmartLink App.** This app lets your parole officer connect with you without having to come to your house.

Be careful with apps. Use careful judgment about what you'd like to keep private. Be aware that apps can use up your phone data.

# Social Media

Many people stay in touch with others and get news through social media. Social media websites and apps allow people to talk and share photos. Some social media sites are used mostly for friends and family while others are used for jobs. Here are two popular social media platforms:

- **Facebook** is the most popular social media company in the US. People use this site to share photos, updates, and articles. It helps people stay in touch with family and friends; others use it for work. You can comment publicly on posts created by others or message users individually. You can also join Facebook groups to meet other people and get support. Signing up for Facebook is free. To sign up, download the app or type facebook.com into the search bar, and then click "Create Account."
- **LinkedIn** is a social network created for finding jobs. You can use it to talk with employers and share your resume. To create an account, download the app or type linkedin.com into your web browser, and then click "Join Now." Search "How to Create a LinkedIn Account Wikihow" to learn more.

## Staying Safe on Social Media

Be careful when sharing information on Facebook or other social media apps. You can change the privacy settings so that only your friends see your posts. Public posts can be accessed by parole officers and employers. Also remember that the information that you see on social media may not be trustworthy. It's a good idea to check with other sources.

# Video Conferencing

Many people use video conferencing to talk to family, friends, and co-workers. With video conferencing, you can talk to multiple people at the same time and see people's faces. Video conferencing apps can be a great way to stay connected to family members and friends. Lots of meetings these days aren't in person; instead, they use video conferencing. Many job interviews also use video conferencing. You will need to set up an account with the platform (Zoom, Skype, etc.) before the interview.

Common video conferencing options include Facetime, Google Meet, Skype, and Zoom. If you have a computer or phone you can download these apps for their video conferencing services. Most are free.

In most cases, you will be a guest in a video conferencing meeting. This means you will get an invitation in your email with a link that says "Click to Join." When the webpage opens in your web browser, you may join via the app or your web browser. There may also be an option to call in with your phone.

**Video conferencing etiquette tips:**
- If you are in a group, mute yourself when you're not talking (click on the microphone).
- Be aware of your appearance and background. If you do not want people to see you, you can turn your camera off by clicking the camera icon. If you want people to see you but not your living space, you can use a "virtual background." For job interviews, it is important to have your camera on, your lighting good, and your background clear of distractions.

# Digital Literacy Resources

Learning technology is a lot like learning a new language, but there are many free learning resources.

- **Techboomers.com** is a free website that teaches people basic computer skills to help them improve their quality of life. You can learn about helpful websites, social media, online shopping, and technology basics.

- **Netliteracy.org** has resources and training on everything from basic email and social media to artificial intelligence.

- **Northstar**, at digitalliteracyassessment.org , will test your skills and help you learn more.

# Reflect

1. What will I need to use technology for after my reentry? What will I want to use technology for?

2. What technologies do I know how to use?

3. What will I need help with?

4. Can my friends and family help me learn? Where else can I go for help?

Mapping Your Future, National Edition

# Legal Matters

After you are released, there may be times when you need to go to court or get legal help. For example, you might want to get your record sealed so you can get a better job. Maybe you want to get back custody of a child.

This chapter covers the following topics:
- Getting Legal Help
- Child Custody
- Child Support
- Fees and Fines
- Expunging or Sealing Records
- Certificates of Rehabilitation
- Executive Clemency

☆ Please note that we are not lawyers and do not provide legal advice. We try our best to help you understand your legal options. Ask a lawyer if you need more help.

## Getting Legal Help

**Pro bono.** Figuring out the courts can be frustrating. It's best to get the help of a lawyer. Lawyers understand the rules and know how local judges and courtrooms work. Lawyers are often expensive, but there are lawyers who will work on your case for free (pro bono). These services are available through legal aid programs. Begin your search for a legal aid office near you here: www.lawhelp.org. The Justice Department offers this list of pro bono help for immigration issues: www.justice.gov/eoir/list-pro-bono-legal-service-providers .

**Pro se.** Some cases can be handled without lawyers. Things like sealing criminal records, family law, and small claims matters often don't use lawyers. This is cheaper, but it is almost always better to hire a lawyer or find one who will work for free.

**Pro se help desks.** If you decide to file pro se, most counties offer pro se help desks. The service is free. There are workers who can help you with pro se forms, courthouse directions, and legal consultations. Call your county circuit clerk's office for information.

## Child Custody

Child custody responsibilities vary by state. In general, they involve:

- **Parental responsibilities:** If you have parental responsibilities, it means you can make choices about your child's future, like where they go to school.
- **Parenting time:** If you have parenting time, it means you can spend time with your child. The court will decide how much time you can spend together. Even if you don't have parental responsibilities, you can still have a good amount of parenting time.

Custody can be complicated. Many people hire a lawyer to help. If you choose not to have a lawyer, you will need to file a petition to modify custody. Petitions can be found online or by visiting your county's circuit clerk office. There will usually be a fee. Once you have filed your petition and the court has read it, the court should set a date for a hearing to change custody.

The laws around filing for child custody without a lawyer vary widely from state to state. This page at the VeryWellFamily website offers useful advice at the national level and provides advice on finding state-level information as well: tinyurl.com/pro-se-custody .

## Foster Care and Reinstating Parental Rights

What if your child is in foster care or with a relative? What if your parental rights have been terminated? You may still be able to get your rights restored. The first step is understanding how the process works. The second step is understanding where you are in your own case.

After your case has started, your state's department of children and family services may remove your child from your home. If this happens, the department will try to place your child with family members, or people who serve as family members. The department may not know of all your family members, so let them know if there is someone who can help that they don't know about. (**Note**: In Florida, this department is called the Department of Children and Families [DCF]; in Illinois and Alaska, it is the Department of Children and Family Services [DCFS]; in Tennessee, it is the Department of Children's Services [DCS]. Your state's department may have a different name.)

If you have lost custody of your child, your child was assigned a caseworker whose job it is to protect their best interests. Speaking with this caseworker can be a good place to start. You will also need a lawyer. Let the judge in your case know if you can't afford a lawyer. The judge will assign one to you.

DCFS has to try to help you get your child back. They will give you a list of things you need to do for your child to come home. This list may include:

- Parenting classes
- Counseling
- Continuing education
- Anger management
- Drug or alcohol classes
- Minor changes to your home

You will have to show the judge and DCFS that you are making "reasonable efforts" and "reasonable progress" to finish everything on the list.

It is very difficult to show you are making reasonable efforts while incarcerated, but it is not impossible. It is important to try to do the things on your DCFS list as well as you can. Try to keep records of this for your lawyer.

Once you leave prison, you can work to finish your list. DCFS must give you a fair chance to complete their list. But the judge is the one who decides whether you get your child back.

If your child is out of your care for a certain amount of time (15 months in Illinois), the judge can terminate your parental rights. This means you would not be your child's legal parent anymore.

If you no longer have parental rights, it is possible to get them back. But it may be hard. You can file something called a motion to reinstate your rights. You can hire a lawyer to do this or do it yourself.

## Child Support

If you don't live with your child, you may need to pay child support. Child support is money that you pay to the person who is taking care of your child. Child support lasts until children turn 18, or 19 if they are still in high school. You will pay a certain amount of your income in child support. The amount you pay depends on how many children you have and your income level. A judge may order you to pay for other things too, like healthcare, child care, or school costs.

### Reducing Payments

It is very important to pay your child support. If you don't pay, you might have money taken out of your paycheck. You may be able to get your payments lowered if you:

- Are suddenly making less money
- Are incarcerated
- Have large healthcare costs

If one of these things happens to you, you need to let the court know as soon as you can. You'll need to file a petition with the court. You can hire a lawyer to do this or do it yourself. Once you file the petition, you'll probably need to go to court to talk about your case.

If a court has ordered a suspension of your driver's license for failure to pay child support, it is important to petition to reduce that payment. Many judges allow you to make payments according to your income.

## Getting Payments You are Owed

Are you getting child support? If your childcare expenses have gone up, you can ask for more support from your child's other parent. Changes in childcare expenses can come from things like:

- Medical bills for the child
- New education expenses
- A big change in your household's cost of living

If the other parent recently started making a lot more money, you can also ask for more support.

If you are not getting the child support payments you believe you are owed, contact your state's child support enforcement office.

## Fees and Fines

There are many different legal fees and fines you may have to pay:

- Traffic tickets
- DUI fees
- Payments to the victims of the crime you were convicted of
- Other fines related to the crime
- Fines and debt for failing to pay child support
- Parole or probation fines, such as fees for anger management or parenting classes and fees for any required registration

Even small fees can make it hard to get back on your feet. Still, it's important to plan for how you will pay them. Not paying your fees or fines can get you in more trouble.

- Officials can hold those fees against you if you return to jail.
- Sometimes people are returned to jail for not paying fees, especially if they "willfully" do not pay them.
- Sometimes fees have a high interest rate, meaning the amount you owe will get larger the longer you wait to pay.

*It's hard to make a decision between paying fines and staying out of jail, or paying bills and having somewhere to live.*

**—Anonymous**

But there is good news. There are programs that can help you with your fees.

**Waivers for court fees.** In some states, there is a waiver program for court costs for people who live significantly below the poverty level. Check with your state to see if a waiver program exists.

**Removal of past child support debt.** Check in your state to see if this is an option. In Illinois, for instance, the Clean Slate program removes your child support debt if you agree to pay regular child support payments moving forward.

## Expunging or Sealing Records

Sealing your record means employers can't see your record. This could make it easier to find a job. Ask your parole officer or reentry organization to see if this is an option for you. You may be able to get your record sealed once you are off of parole, depending on the charge. Some states even have automatic record clearing for certain convictions.

Sometimes it is also possible to get a record expunged. An expunged record is erased. This means nobody can see it anymore. This usually only happens if your charges were dismissed.

# Certificates of Rehabilitation

These are official documents that can restore rights you lost because of your conviction. Certificates of rehabilitation can allow you to apply for jobs that require licenses issued by the state. These jobs include work in childcare, education, and transit. Depending on your state, they can also restore your right to serve on a jury.

These certificates have different names and different purposes in different states. Check to see if your state offers certificates of rehabilitation, what they require, and what they can do.

# Executive Clemency

You may also be able to petition the governor for executive clemency or a pardon. This is another way to attempt to remove the barriers in your way after incarceration. You will need to explain why you are seeking a pardon, including opportunities that were denied to you because of your criminal record. You can also submit character-reference letters from friends and family and former teachers and employers. You will likely have the right to a hearing, but we can't say what's true in your particular state. Do your research. Many people chose to hire a lawyer to represent them in this process.

# Finances, Credit, and Taxes

Thinking about money can be stressful. Take small steps toward managing your money, especially if you're doing it on your own for the first time. Having control over your finances will help you avoid money troubles in the long run. It will help you take control of your life and feel more secure about the future.

This chapter covers the following topics:
- Banking Basics
- Using Bank Cards for Purchases
- Budgeting and Financial Resources
- Avoiding Scams
- Credit
- Filing Taxes

 ## Banking Basics

It's a good idea to open a bank account so that you have a safe place to put your money. A bank account also helps you avoid the fees that come with cashing checks and transfering money.

There are two basic types of bank accounts: checking and savings accounts. A **checking account** keeps your money safe. It also gives you easy access to your money so you can buy things and pay bills. When you open a checking account, you get checks and a debit card. You can use these to buy things, pay bills, or get cash from your account using ATMs. Some checking accounts have monthly fees while others do not, so make sure you ask about fees.

Once you have some money saved, it's a good idea to open a **savings account**. A savings account allows you to earn more interest on your money. This means that if you leave the money in your savings account, it grows over time (usually at a very slow pace). You cannot write checks from a savings account, but some savings accounts will allow you to access your money through an ATM.

There are many good reasons to have a bank account:
- Putting your paychecks in a bank account is cheaper than paying fees for check cashing services.
- Some employers put your earnings directly in your account. This is called "direct deposit."
- If you have a debit card, you don't need to carry lots of cash.
- Many banks offer free access to online banking services, which you can use to keep track of your money, pay bills automatically, and transfer money between accounts.
- Smartphone apps like Venmo let you transfer and receive money without any fees. You can get Venmo on your phone and use it if you have a bank account.
- You can work with your bank to get car or mortgage loans, develop a retirement investment plan, and invest in stocks.

You don't have to be a U.S. citizen or have a Social Security number to open a bank account. You can open an account using the Individual Taxpayer Identification Number (ITIN) assigned to you by the IRS, regardless of immigration status. Visit IRS.gov for more information about ITINs.

# Choosing a Bank

Banks and credit unions offer different products to choose from, like checking and savings accounts, loans, rewards programs, and credit cards. Before choosing a bank, think about what you need. When you first go to the bank, ask to speak to someone who can help you understand their services and how they can meet your needs.

Here are a few things to consider:

- Is the bank local, or does it have ATMs and branches in other cities? If you plan to travel a lot, you may want to choose a bank that has many locations. Online banks are also an option.
- What fees does the bank have? Look out for overdraft fees (when you take out more money than you have), fees for closing accounts, fees for foreign transactions, and monthly maintenance fees.
- Does your employer, school, or community have a credit union? Credit unions are better in some ways than banks. See the chart below comparing banks and credit unions.
- Has a bank ever shut down your checking account? If so, banks might reject your account application. Don't worry though, because some banks offer second-chance checking accounts. Call and ask smaller local banks and credit unions about their account policies. They may be more open to people who have had financial trouble.
- Is your bank or credit union backed by the government? If it is, that means that if the bank closes or has other problems, your money is protected. Make sure your bank is a member of the FDIC or NCUA.
- Are you a veteran? If so, you qualify for a USAA account. USAA members and their families can often get good rates on loans. Visit usaa.com for more information.
- Do you have bad credit? Many banks use a database called ChexSystems to check your bank customer history, but they don't always pull your credit report when you apply. Ask them about their policies.

|  | **Banks** | **Credit Unions** |
|---|---|---|
| **Pros** | • Easier to open an account<br>• Many branches and ATM locations<br>• More options for types of accounts, loans, and credit cards<br>• Online banking and services | • Not-for-profit institutions<br>• Member owned<br>• Smaller, with better customer service<br>• Higher interest on savings accounts<br>• Lower rates for loans<br>• More flexibility |
| **Cons** | • More restrictions<br>• Less flexible if you make an error<br>• Higher interest rates on loans and credit cards<br>• Owned by investors who may not act in your best interest | • More exclusive memberships<br>• Fewer locations<br>• Fewer product options (loans, etc.)<br>• Less online service |

 # Using Bank Cards for Purchases

If you've been in prison for a long time, buying things at the store may look very different. Perhaps you carried around cash in the past or wrote paper checks. Most people these days use debit cards or credit cards rather than paying with cash or checks.

Here are some card options:
- With a credit card, you are borrowing money and will need to pay it back. We talk more about credit cards in the next section.
- Debit cards look just like credit cards but work differently. Most debit cards are linked to a checking account, and they only let you spend money that you already have in that account. Debit cards can be used wherever credit cards are accepted. You can also use your debit card to get cash from an ATM.
- With prepaid debit cards, you can load money onto the card when you get it. Then you use it to make purchases. Prepaid debit cards are often used by people who can't get a bank account. You might use one if you haven't been able to get your ID yet. Bluebird and Chime are prepaid debit cards with no monthly fee.
- Gift cards work like prepaid debit cards. Some cards—like a Visa Gift Card—can be used at any store, while other gift cards only work for specific stores.
- Many states offer EBT (Electronic Benefits Transfer) cards for food stamps and/or cash benefits. You can use these cards just like a debit card at stores that accept EBT.

For debit cards, you will need to make a 4-digit PIN number, which is like a password. Before you use your card, make sure you have your PIN number set up. Usually, there is a phone number on the back of the card that you can call to set up the PIN number. When using a debit card or EBT card, make sure you know how much money you have. If you don't have enough money, your card may not work.

*The first time I went to the store by myself, I got up to the front of the line and didn't know how to pay for my groceries. I saw this contraption for a card that looked real complicated and didn't know how to use it. A long line of people were behind me and getting restless when I was just standing there looking dumbfounded. I didn't want to tell anyone I had been locked up and didn't know how to use a link or debit card. I was embarrassed and panicked!*

**—Michael**

It can be embarrassing if you don't know how to use a card. Here's a brief guide (summarized from the Wikihow website) about what to expect when you check out at a store.

1. After the cashier scans your things, they will ask you to pay.
2. There will likely be a card reader on the counter. Card readers look a little bit like calculators. They usually have a screen with instructions to follow.
3. The screen on the card reader may ask if you agree to pay the amount on the screen. You may have to press "enter" or "yes" to continue.
4. Next, the screen may ask you to swipe your card. Other times, the cashier will let you know when the machine is ready for you to swipe your card.
5. Some card readers will need you to swipe your card on the right side. Others will need you to stick your card into a slot and leave it there. Don't worry if you don't get it right the first time. Lots of people have to swipe their cards a few times. Everyone needs to ask the cashier for help sometimes.
6. Some modern card readers may ask you to "tap" your card. This means that you lay your card down on the chip reader instead of inserting or swiping it. This only works with some cards. This may seem confusing, but remember that cashiers are used to offering help.
7. The card reader may ask whether you want to pay by "debit" or "credit." If you hit debit, it may ask you to enter your 4-digit PIN number. Once the screen says "Approved" you should get a receipt. You can take your items and your receipt and leave.
8. Some debit cards allow you to get "cash back" with your purchase. This is like an ATM withdrawal. The card reader screen will ask if you want cash, and you will enter the dollar amount you would like. The cashier will then give you the cash. The amount will come out of your bank account with no additional fees charged.
9. If you are using a credit card, you may be asked to sign a paper receipt or sign the screen with a special pen that is attached to the card reader. It will ask you to press "enter" or "accept" when you are finished. Once you have finished signing and get your receipt, you should be ready to go.

**Learn more about how to use a debit card here:** wikihow.life/Use-a-Debit-Card .
**Learn about how to use an ATM here:** wikihow.com/Use-an-ATM .

**Remember:** It's OK to ask for help! Lots of people have problems using their cards. The cashiers are there to help you, and they are used to doing so.

# Budgeting and Financial Resources

One of the easiest things you can do to manage your money is to make a budget. Budgeting can help you know where your money is going so you do not spend more than you make. There are thousands of different budget forms you can download online for free. Budget apps for your phone allow you to track purchases as you make them. To make your own budget, add up how much money you make every month. Then, make a list of everything you spend money on in a month and compare the two numbers.

You can find information online about banks, credit unions, account options, and strategies for saving your money. Some financial planning websites let you ask an advisor a question and get an answer right away. Here are some resources for help with money:

| | |
|---|---|
| Free budgeting app | www.ramseysolutions.com/ramseyplus/everydollar |
| Budgeting and understanding money | thesimpledollar.com |
| Budgeting, banking, credit, financial planning, mortgages, and insurance | nerdwallet.com |
| Budgeting, personal finance, credit, and more | annuity.org , annuity.org/financial-literacy , annuity.org/annuities/types/income |
| Financial planning | learnvest.com , mint.com |
| One-stop-shop finance education and advice | - Finance at Khan Academy: www.khanacademy.org/economics-finance-domain/core-finance<br>- CNN's Money 101: money.cnn.com/pf/money-essentials<br>- The Federal Financial Literacy and Education Commission's site: MyMoney.gov<br>- For a longer (but older) list of popular financial-advice websites, visit businessinsider.com/best-websites-money-advice-2014-12 |

☆ **Disclaimer:** Please remember that we are not telling you you must use any of these websites or services. The resources listed here are suggestions. It is important to think, on your own, about any advice you are given.

# Avoiding Scams

You don't want to become a victim of a scam. Visit this website for a list of common scams and their warning signs: fbi.gov/scams-and-safety/common-scams-and-crimes .

There are always new scams to be aware of. In addition to the FBI site, the Better Business Bureau Scam Tracker (www.bbb.org/scamtracker) and the Federal Trade Commission (consumer.ftc.gov/scams) both have information on many of the latest scams. They also let you report if you've been a victim of a scam.

*Here are a few ways to avoid getting scammed:*

- Be suspicious of emails or calls that offer you lots of money or "free gifts" if you pay a small fee. If the reward sounds too good to be true, avoid it.
- Beware of companies that try to push you into signing up for something immediately. Only sign up for services you understand. If you ask for more information and they become impatient or don't answer your question, do not trust them.
- Only give personal information (such as account and Social Security numbers or your birthday) to companies you know to be trustworthy.
- Never pay for a letter of credit.

# Credit

You may be considering getting a credit card so that you can buy things with credit. Buying on credit means that you buy things now and pay for them later. A bank or credit card company loans you the money, and you agree to repay them later. Usually, this means that you buy something with your credit card, and then you make monthly payments to the bank until the loan is repaid.

When you buy with credit, you must pay interest. Interest is a fee for borrowing the money. A loan's interest rate determines how much interest you will owe every month. High interest rates can be very expensive. Think hard before you get any credit card, and make sure not to sign up for too many. The more cards you have, the more payments you will have to make. Also, having too many credit cards will damage your credit score. A bad credit score will make banks want to charge you more interest. Credit card companies make money when people get deeper and deeper into debt. You do not want to be that customer!

A credit counselor at a nonprofit organization can give you good advice about getting a credit card. One example is credit.org, which offers free telephone counseling sessions.

Sometimes, credit cards can lead to a lot of trouble. If you buy too much with credit cards, it can be hard to pay your monthly payments. A service like credit.org can help you figure things out if you get overwhelmed. To be safe, only buy with your credit card what you can pay for within a month.

It's different for major purchases, like a car, a house, or college tuition. In these cases, getting a loan makes sense. You may be unable to pay for a car all at once, but the cost becomes easier if you can spread it out over many months. Make sure to choose a car that is affordable, so that you can manage your monthly payments. Try to get a loan with an interest rate that is as low as possible. Again, be cautious and talk to a credit counselor before going into debt.

If you decide to get a credit card or buy something using credit, your bank will first look at your credit score (also called your credit rating). A credit score is a number that tells them whether they think you will repay a loan. If you have a good credit score, it will be easier to get loans and lower interest rates. If you were in debt before you went to prison, you will need to take steps to improve your credit score. Credit scores range from 300 (bad credit) to 850 (excellent credit).

Here are some guidelines for managing credit:

**Get educated.** Being uninformed can lead to costly mistakes. For a good primer on your credit score, check out this website: www.consumerfinance.gov/consumer-tools/credit-reports-and-scores .

**Be smart.** Avoid businesses (such as car dealerships and payday loan offices) that advertise directly to people with bad credit. They often have extremely high interest rates. Their business depends on your failure to pay your debts on time. Do not support any company whose business model depends on your lack of money.

**Be cautious.** Read the fine print carefully and understand the rules before you sign anything. Remember, what counts is what is in the contract, not what the salesperson promised.

**Pay your debts.** If you've gotten behind on any of your debts—or have had debts fall into collections—pay them, or make a plan for starting to pay them. For information about managing debt, see this website: consumer.ftc.gov/articles/coping-debt .

**Pay your bills on time.** Paying on time is a good habit and can improve your credit score. The easiest way to do that is by setting up an automatic payment with your bank on your bills' due dates. Marking the dates on a calendar is fine, too.

**Use credit cards wisely.** If you choose to have a credit card, don't charge what you can't pay back at the end of the month. If you must borrow money with a credit card to pay your credit card bills, it's time to talk with a credit counselor.

*If possible I would suggest you have a loved one that you trust and who believes in you to add you to some line of credit much like parents do for their children. Trust me, you will need it.*

**—Shaun**

*Open a bank account. Work on building up your credit. If you get a credit card, use less than 30% of the credit limit, buy things with your credit card, and then use the 30 day grace period to pay the bill in its entirety. That's the slow way to build credit.*

**—JoeJoe**

# Filing Taxes

Once you start earning money, you will have to pay federal and state taxes. You must file your taxes every year. The amount you pay depends on how much you make and who lives with you. Things like childcare, disability, and healthcare costs will also change how much you pay. Taxes are taken out of your paycheck.

When you file taxes, you let the government know how much you have earned and how much you have paid in taxes. You can also tell them things like if you have children, disability, or healthcare costs. The government decides whether you have paid too much or too little in taxes. In many cases, you will find that you have paid too much, and you will get a tax refund. If you have paid too little, you have to pay the amount you owe. If you do not file your taxes, you won't receive a refund, you will have to pay a fee, and you may owe back taxes. Depending on where you live, this may also be a violation of parole.

**W-4 Form: Claiming Incoming and Exemptions.** When you start a new job, you are asked to fill out an IRS Form W-4. This form helps your employer know how much of your paycheck should be withheld for taxes. It is important to fill out this form so that you can arrange to pay taxes month by month. If you don't fill it out, you'll have to pay them all at once at the end of the year. To learn how to fill out a W-4 form, visit the following website: wikihow.com/Fill-Out-a-W-4 .

**Filing Taxes.** Every year, you will need to file both federal and state taxes by April 15. Many people choose to file their taxes in January so that they can get their tax refund sooner.

To file taxes, you will need a W-2 form from your employer(s). Employers will usually give you W-2 forms in January. Next, you will need to decide which type of tax return to complete. Some of the more common forms are:

- Form 1040 (US Individual Income Tax Return)
- Form 1040A (US Individual Income Tax Return)
- Form 1040EZ (Income Tax Return for Single and Joint Filers With No Dependents)
- Form 1040NR (US Nonresident Alien Income Tax Return)
- Form 1040NR-EZ (US Income Tax Return for Certain Nonresident Aliens With No Dependents)

Because filing taxes can be confusing, many people get help from a tax professional called a certified public accountant, or CPA.

Simply bring your W-2s and any other IRS forms to their office. For a fee, they will file your taxes for you. This means you won't have to worry about mistakes or spending a lot of time on your taxes. This is a good idea for people who have multiple jobs or other complicated tax situations. If you are looking for a CPA, ask someone you trust to recommend one.

There are also online websites that can help you file your taxes. These websites cost less than a tax professional. If you have a simple tax situation, you might want to use a website. The website will guide you through your return using a series of questions and automatic calculations. Remember to read all instructions and offers carefully. It should be free to file your federal tax return, but most online services charge to file your state tax return. Some of the most popular online tax-filing websites are:

- e-file.com
- freetaxusa.com
- turbotax.intuit.com
- hrblock.com
- taxact.com
- jacksonhewitt.com

Some places offer free tax help for people. See this website to check if there is a program near you: irs.gov/individuals/free-tax-return-preparation-for-qualifying-taxpayers .

# Voting

Voting rights for people with felony convictions vary by state. In a few states, you don't lose your right to vote at all and can vote from prison. In others, you have the right to vote after release. In some states, you can vote after you are released from prison and finish your parole or probation. Finally, in a few states, you may not ever be able to vote, or you may have to pay all your fines before you can vote. See the table below.

| May vote from prison | Vote restored after prison | Vote restored after prison, parole, and probation | May lose vote permanently (or have additional requirements to meet) |
|---|---|---|---|
| District of Columbia, Maine, Puerto Rico, Vermont | California, Colorado, Connecticut, Hawaii, Illinois, Indiana, Maryland, Massachusetts, Michigan, Montana, Nevada, New Hampshire, New Jersey, New York, North Dakota, Ohio, Oregon, Pennsylvania, Rhode Island, Utah, Washington | Alaska, Arkansas, Georgia, Idaho, Kansas, Louisiana, Minnesota, Missouri, New Mexico, North Carolina, Oklahoma, South Carolina, South Dakota, Texas, West Virginia, Wisconsin | Alabama, Arizona, Delaware, Florida, Iowa, Kentucky, Mississippi, Nebraska, Tennessee, Virginia, Wyoming |

The ACLU provides this map with the most current information: tinyurl.com/aclu-voting-map .

Taking voting rights away from people with felonies is known as "felony disenfranchisement." This practice damages our democracy and has deep roots in Jim Crow-era racism. According to the Sentencing Project, it "weakens the political power of communities of color" and, in 2022, over 4.6 million Americans with felony convictions were not allowed to vote.

System-impacted activists, advocates, and allies are successfully fighting to pass laws that take back lost voting rights, but they still have a long way to go. The Sentencing Project explains this in more detail and shows how it may affect the right to vote in your state here: tinyurl.com/Sentencingproject-vote .

**So, if you can vote, you should! Your vote matters.** Your vote can make a difference, especially at the local and state levels.

US federal elections (for US President, US Senators, and US Congress Representatives) happen every two or four years, on the first Tuesday in November. State and local elections can take place in any year, at any time. During any federal, state or local elections, you may be voting for state leaders, county or state attorneys, local officials, and sometimes judges. There may be other important offices and issues on the ballot.

# Step 1: Register to Vote.

Each state makes its own voting and election rules, including when and how to register. Learn more at www.usa.gov/register-to-vote, or call (866) OUR-VOTE [(866) 687-8683], a year-round hotline run by the national, nonpartisan Election Protection Coalition. They work "to ensure that all voters have an equal opportunity to vote and have that vote count."

Here are a few common ways to register:
- **Online.** In 42 states, plus D.C., you can register at vote.gov.
- **By mail.** Download the National Mail Voter Registration Form and mail it in. Find the form and instructions here: www.eac.gov/voters/national-mail-voter-registration-form . A librarian can help you download or print the form.
- **In person.** Sometimes you can register to vote at a state or local election office, a DMV, or a place where you sign up for SNAP/food stamps.

In some states, you can register at the polling location on election day. Figure out the options and deadlines in your state as early as you can.

**What do I need to bring to register?** It depends on the state you live in. At a minimum, you will need to write down your name, mailing address, date of birth, telephone number, and ID number (state ID, driver's license, or Social Security number).

Some states require that you show two forms of ID and have a document that shows your name and address (bank statement, government check, utility bill). Be prepared. Call (866) OUR-VOTE [(866) 687-8683] to get details and ask questions.

**When should you register?** You can register at any time, but if you want to vote in an upcoming election, find the registration deadline for your state. Some states require people to register four weeks before the election. In other states, you can register at the voting place on election day.

# Step 2: Learn About the Candidates and Issues.

This guide cannot tell you how to vote. But you can learn about candidates and issues by listening to the news, talking with people you trust, and looking up candidates and issues online. You can also find voter guides and ratings for judges online.

# Step 3: Vote!

Depending on your state, you may be required to show your ID to vote. Bring your voter registration card and ID with you just in case. Normally, there are two ways that you can vote:
- In person, on election day or during an early-voting period.
- By mail-in ballot. Contact your election authority or call (866) OUR-VOTE [(866) 687-8683] if you need help requesting a mail-in ballot.

You can bring notes, voting guides, and this voter information into the voting booth. It's a good idea to do this, because there can be a lot to remember.

Take your time. Do not let anyone rush you. If you need help, ask a poll worker. They cannot tell you who or what to vote for, but they can answer questions about the process. They can help you read and mark a ballot if you have difficulty reading or if your English is limited. You can also request a ballot in other languages.

Call (866) OUR-VOTE [(866) 687-8683] if you run into any problems while voting.

# Veterans

This section on VA (Veterans Administration) benefits and services covers the following topics:

- Transferring Benefits to Your Family
- Reinstating Benefits After Release
- Filing Disability Claims
- Health
- Housing
- Employment

Once you are released, there are many veteran programs and benefits that can help you. If you have questions we don't discuss here, or if you need assistance with these benefits and services, contact a VA representative by calling (800) 393-0865 or searching for your state's VA benefits office.

In general, you will not be able to receive your VA pension while you are incarcerated. After you go to prison, you will still get your benefits for 60 days. After that time, you may still get the checks, but you will have to return the money to the VA.

If you have an injury or disability that is 80 to 100% related to your military service, you can receive 10% of your pension while incarcerated. You cannot receive any of your pension for injuries or disabilities that happened after your service.

Veterans who are incarcerated can still get other benefits, including education, training, healthcare, insurance, and burial services. For more information on how the VA serves system-impacted vets, go here: www.benefits.va.gov/PERSONA/veteran-incarcerated.asp .

# Transferring Benefits to Your Family

While you can't get your benefits in prison, you can transfer your pension to your family. This includes a spouse, children, or parents who rely on you for money. They must have financial need to get the benefits. This is called "apportionment."

You (or an adult you are giving your benefits to) should apply for apportionment within one year of the day you were incarcerated. To apply, mail a letter to your VA Regional Office (VARO). Your letter should say who you are and whom you want to transfer your benefits to. You must also complete and mail VA Form 21-0788. There are three ways you can get this form:

1. Ask a prison counselor for assistance. They may be able to get the form for you.
2. Ask someone on the outside to download the form from the website below: https://www.vba.va.gov/pubs/forms/VBA-21-0788-ARE.pdf
3. Tear out and use the form in the back of this book (see p. 159).

**Female Veterans.** VA Medical Centers have program managers who help female veterans. They offer help with VA benefits and healthcare. Contact the closest VA Medical Center to find a program manager who specializes in female veterans.

If you have questions about the process, ask someone you trust to call the Department of Veterans Affairs at (800) 827-1000.

Once the VA gets your application, they will review it. They may ask your spouse or children's guardian to fill out the same form. They will let you know if the apportionment is approved, and your family will retroactively receive your benefits. That means that your benefits will be saved and given to them, starting 60 days after your incarceration. In other words, if your application is accepted, you or your family will eventually receive all of the money you deserve.

# Reinstating Benefits After Release

You can restart your benefits 30 days before your scheduled release. If you are in prison, ask your counselor or someone on the outside to help you contact the Department of Veteran Affairs to get your benefits restored. They can call (800) 393-0865 or go to va.gov for help.

The VA has a reentry program called Health Care for Reentry Veterans (HCRV). They offer:
1. Post-release assessments
2. Referrals to medical, psychiatric, and social services, including employment services and housing assistance
3. Short-term case management after reentry

All major VA Medical Centers (sometimes called "parent facilities") have reentry staff. Contact the closest VA Medical Center to begin receiving services.

You can find VA hospitals and clinics in your state here: https://www.va.gov/directory/guide/allstate.asp .

# Filing Disability Claims

Do you have a disability related to your military service? You can file a disability claim online or in person. You can get disability benefits in prison and once you are released.

To file a claim online, visit the website www.ebenefits.va.gov/ebenefits/apply and create an eBenefits account by clicking "Register." You will need to provide some personal information to open an account. Then click "Apply for Disability Compensation" to apply.

You will need your medical records and any other proof of disability for your claim. You can also apply for a disability claim by filling out a paper application at a VA facility or mailing the claim to a VA facility. You can find VA facilities by visiting: www.va.gov/find-locations . Check out this website to learn how to file a claim: www.va.gov/disability/how-to-file-claim .

The VA does not accept all claims. In fact, they reject almost all claims the first time. Keep trying. The process can be complicated, so you may wish to get help from a Veterans Service Organization (such help is free). Some veterans hire a claims agent or an attorney. You can for search any of these options at this website: www.ebenefits.va.gov/ebenefits/vso-search .

# Health

After you leave prison, you can get care at VA Medical Centers. You can enroll in their system by visiting a VA Medical Center, or by phone at: (877) 222- VETS [(877) 222-8387].

You can only receive care if you were honorably (or generally) discharged. You can receive treatment for injuries unconnected to your military service.

Not all VA healthcare is free. Your insurance will be billed for care, but you will have to pay for part of your inpatient, outpatient, or extended (nursing home) care and medication costs. Some of these services may be free if your income is below a certain limit or if your illness is connected to your service. For more on eligibility, go to www.va.gov/health-care/eligibility .

The VA also offers mental health and substance abuse treatment at VA Medical Centers or at Vet Centers (depending on the treatment). www.va.gov/health/vamc for a list of VA Medical Centers in your state.

# Housing

The VA's Health Care for Homeless Veterans (HCHV) program provides help for veterans who are experiencing homelessness (as does the Homeless Veterans Reintegration Project—see the next section). This includes help accessing your benefit and finding housing. Contact the closest VA Medical Center to get services or learn more here: www.va.gov/homeless/hchv.asp .

**For more information:** Homeless Outreach Coordinator are ready to assist system-impacted Veterans at every VA Regional Office. They can help you learn what benefits you qualify for, help you apply for those benefits, and refer you to other resources as needed. Call the VA's National Call Center for Homeless Veterans at 1-877-4AID-VET (1-877-424-3838) to be connected with a Coordinator in your area.

# Employment

The VA also has employment help for veterans who were honorably (or generally) discharged.

Local Veterans Employment Representatives (LVER) and Disabled Veterans Outreach Program Representatives (DVOP) help veterans find jobs. They also provide job training. You can get help here: https://www.va.gov/careers-employment/.

The Homeless Veterans' Reintegration Project (HVRP) helps unhoused veterans with:

- Access to housing
- Job searches
- Vocational counseling
- Occupational-skills training
- On-the-job training
- Trade-skills certification and licensing
- Job-placement assistance
- Referral to other supportive services

Vocational Rehabilitation and Employment Services assists veterans with disabilities related to their military service. They offer help with job training, job placement, and employment advice. To connect with this program, call (800) 827-1000 or visit www.benefits.gov/benefit/296 .

Veterans Industries and Compensated Work Therapy programs help veterans experiencing homelessness or near-homelessness with any problems they may have with addiction or their physical and/or mental health. These programs contract with businesses to provide paid work for these veterans. They are sometimes housed within VA Medical Centers. For more information go to www.va.gov/health/cwt .

# LGBTQ+ People

If you are a part of the LGBTQ+ community, you may face unique experiences and challenges as you leave prison, and certainly in prison as well. Remember that you're not alone! There are organizations that help LGBTQ+ people.

This chapter covers the following topics:
- Housing
- Employment
- Healthcare and Mental Health
- Substance Use
- Resources for Transgender and Gender-Nonconforming People

## Housing

Finding a place to live is one of the most important parts of reentry. Organizations that work with the LGBTQ+ community can help you find safe housing that is respectful of your identity:
- **Sage USA** (www.sageusa.org/what-we-do/national-lgbt-housing-initiative) provides national housing services for LGBTQ+ elders.
- **The National League of Cities** (www.nlc.org/article/2023/06/30/housing-for-lgbtqia) operates shelters in various cities around the US and advocates for LGBTQ+ housing programs.

If you choose to seek private housing, there may be housing laws that protect you from discrimination. Housing and discrimination laws vary by state. Here are some resources to help you know your rights and protect yourself against discrimination:
- **The Movement Advancement Project** provides information on various laws and policy across the US. View their map of LGBTQ+ nondiscrimination laws here: www.lgbtmap.org/equality-maps/non_discrimination_laws .
- **Lambda Legal** provides legal services to the LGBTQ+ community. They also have a free virtual help desk: lambdalegal.org .
- **The US Department of Housing Discrimination and Urban Development** keeps a list of housing discrimination resources relating to the LGBTQ+ community: www.hud.gov/program_offices/fair_housing_equal_opp/housing_discrimination_and_persons_identifying_lgbtq .

Find general information on your rights as a tenant in the Your Legal Rights section of the Housing After Release chapter (see p. 35).

## Employment

Finding a job when you have a record can be hard, especially if you're facing discrimination for your sexuality or gender identity. There are organizations and resources that can help! In addition to the resources listed in our Employment chapter (see p. 40), some organizations provide employment services specifically for LGBTQ+ people:
- **The LGBT Career Resource Guide** provides many resources on finding a job and making sure that employer is LGBTQ+ friendly: www.velvetjobs.com/articles/insights/lgbt-career-resources .
- **Campus Pride** offers a job board and hosts free online training sessions for student members of the LGBTQ+ community: www.campuspride.org . Some of their services are just for current students, but the job listings are available to everyone.

## Healthcare and Mental Health

If you're struggling with your mental health, always remember you're not alone. If you're transgender or gender nonconforming, you can call the Trans Lifeline at (877) 565-8860. If you're 24 or younger,

Mapping Your Future, National Edition

you can call the Trevor Project at (866) 488-7386. Both lifelines are designed to help members of the LGBTQ+ community. Suicide Helpline counselors are trained to help people of all orientations and gender identities. In emergencies, call them at 988.
- **The LGBTQ+ National Help Center** offers free and confidential peer support from volunteer members of the LGBTQ+ community. Reach them at (888) 843-4564 or by visiting www.lgbthotline.org .
- **The World Professional Organization for Transgender Health (WPATH)** has a directory of healthcare providers trained on the needs of the LGBTQ+ community. Search their directory here: www.wpath.org/member/search .
- **AIDS in Prison Project Hotline:** This hotline provides information on HIV and AIDS for people on the inside. They accept collect calls at (718) 378-7022.

Find more resources in the Health and Trauma and Mental Health chapters (see p. 62 & 68), including information on HIV/AIDS, STDs, and sexual and reproductive health.

## Substance Use

If you have trouble controlling your use of drugs or alcohol, we urge you to get help. These support groups welcome people from the LGBTQ+ community:
- **SMART Recovery** hosts support groups and sessions for LGBTQ+ people struggling with substance use. Join groups who meet online or in-person groups here: www.smartrecovery.org/lgbtq .
- **Gay & Sober** provides safe spaces for LGBTQ+ people recovering from addiction. Find meetings and additional resources here: www.gayandsober.org .
- LGBTQ+-focused Alcoholics and Narcotics Anonymous chapters often identify themselves as **Lambda AA** or **Lambda NA .** To find a Lambda group, start here: aa.org/find-aa . Search for your city or county from that website to find a list of local AA networks. Select the network nearest to you, and then, to find your local LAMBDA chapter, select LGBTQ+ from the "meeting type" menu.

You can find more general resources in the Substance Use chapter (see p. 76).

## Transgender and Gender Nonconforming People

### Changing Your Name
Policies for changing your name vary by state. Some states require you to live there for a certain amount of time. Others have additional restrictions for people on specific registries or with felony convictions. The National Center for Transgender Equality has created an ID Documents Center where you can search by state for how to change your name and/or gender marker on your state ID. Explore those resources here: transequality.org/documents .

### Hormone Therapy and Gender Affirming Surgery
Talk to your doctor (primary care provider) if you want to start hormone replacement therapy (HRT) or have gender affirming surgery. Sometimes your primary care provider can prescribe hormones, but they will often refer you to a specialist, like an endocrinologist. Some health centers specialize in healthcare for transgender people. Many Planned Parenthood health centers provide access to HRT, gender affirming care, surgery referrals, transition support, and other services important to transgender people. Search for one near you here: www.plannedparenthood.org/get-care/our-services/gender-affirming-care .

**Note:** Not all Planned Parenthood health centers provide all services. Make sure to call and check which services they offer before you make an appointment.

## Other LGBTQ+ Resources

- **CenterLink** is a national association of LGBTQ+ centers and organizations. Find one near you here: www.lgbtqcenters.org/LGBTCenters .
- **The Trevor Project** is a crisis intervention program that operates nationally for young LGBTQ+ people. See their resource directory here: www.thetrevorproject.org/resources .
- **The Human Rights Campaign** advocates for LGBTQ+ equality. See their resource directory here: www.hrc.org/resources .

# Part 3:
# Healing and Moving Forward

- Beginning to Heal
- Building Healthy Relationships
- Mindfulness
- Connecting with Your Community

# Beginning to Heal

Prison hurts in a lot of ways. People who are incarcerated sometimes push others away to protect themselves from that pain. Some people stay away from relationships, grieving, and self-care to stop themselves from feeling helpless. They may become distant and isolated in order to feel safe.

> *My family thinks that because I'm free, all my problems are over, but really we carry all this baggage with us. The coping mechanisms we had on the inside are still with us, and they create barriers on the outside.*
>
> **—Pablo**

Healing is a part of moving forward and reconnecting the pieces of your life. It is a process, and it requires you to be both vulnerable and strong. Being vulnerable is hard. You need to let yourself feel the pain of incarceration. Opening up to yourself and being open to trusting others is a big step toward getting your life back.

Prison is often traumatic, and recovery will take time. Working toward recovery is a form of healing. Vulnerability is not weakness, and it is not weak to ask for help. Support groups and individual counseling can help you deal with trauma that may have happened while you were in prison. See the Trauma and Mental Health chapter (on p. 68) for information on finding support.

This section addresses several aspects of wellness. Understanding them can help you heal and move forward. It is based on suggestions given to us by the system-impacted people who have taken classes through our organization.

What is wellness? Wellness is a complicated subject. It means something different for everyone. After you leave prison, wellness is about making meaning out of your experiences. It also means making these experiences a part of who you are and who you want to be in the world. It is about forgiveness, healing, caring for yourself, and reconnecting with others.

**Emotional wellness** means being respectful of yourself and others. It means you are aware of your good or bad feelings and accept them. You express your feelings to others in healthy and constructive ways. It also means you think about other people's feelings and perspectives. People may think differently than you. Knowing how to disagree respectfully is key to healthy relationships, and healthy relationships are key to emotional wellness. You may have other unresolved issues you're dealing with, such as grief, anger, or depression. Be patient and realize the path to emotional wellness can be a long one.

> *Reach out to somebody. One of our coping mechanisms that's prevalent with individuals who are incarcerated is that we retract ourselves, isolate ourselves to try to deal with it, with the psychological hurdles we're going through.*
>
> **—Pablo**

**Physical wellness** is taking care of your body. It is important to stay active and healthy. Consider finding a gym, jogging, walking, biking, practicing yoga, or looking up free at-home exercise videos online. It's good to eat healthy and drink plenty of water. Practice safe sex by using condoms. For those with addiction issues, getting help through counseling or recovery programs can be a really positive step. You can read more about healthcare in our Health chapter (see p. 62).

**Social wellness** means you look for healthy relationships with many kinds of people. As we discuss in the Building Healthy Relationships chapter (see p. 114), reentry is a time when you will strengthen old relationships and build new ones. While it can be difficult to put yourself out there, it can also lead to meaningful, healthy relationships.

*Advice for socializing outside? Learning coping skills and anger management. Being less abrasive and open-minded.*

**—Earl W.**

**Spiritual wellness** is thinking about a larger meaning or purpose to life. This can, but does not have to, involve religion. You may decide to join a church, synagogue, or mosque. You may also decide to join a support group to find community and purpose. Set aside some time each day to be open, listen, and think about what's going on inside. Practice mindfulness or meditation. The Mindfulness chapter describes a few ways to do this (see p. 126).

*Take a breath. You're going to be in for a ride, and you better pack your patience.*

**—Pablo**

**Occupational wellness** is contributing meaningfully and respectfully in your job. Your job may not be perfect, but how you do it is entirely up to you. What are your strengths? Bring those to your work. Invest in yourself by investing in what you do. Find ways to do a little extra, and try new things when you can. Take the time to realize the value of the work you do, and honor that. Also, beware of toxic work environments. Some jobs can be unhealthy—physically, emotionally, or otherwise. If your job does more harm than good, leaving may be the right choice.

**Environmental wellness** means being aware of Earth's resources and trying to create a healthy environment. There are many ways to contribute. You can grow vegetables in a community garden or volunteer to help with community clean up. Spend time in nature, even if it's at a local park, to help you feel healthy.

*What I felt was most difficult when I first got out is figuring out how to relate to other people. You have both the lack of 'normal' experiences that most people have as late-teenagers and young adults. Plus you have the negative effects of long-term imprisonment.*

**—Greg A.**

# Building Healthy Relationships

Prison makes it hard to stay connected with family, friends, and loved ones. Reentry removes some of these barriers, but it can be a hard time for both you and your loved ones. Rebuilding healthy, positive relationships requires time, patience, and openness. You've changed while in prison, and so have your loved ones. It's going to take time to get to know each other again.

Since you've been gone a long time, you may struggle to feel like you belong. You and your loved ones may feel uncertain about each other. You may wonder if you can trust each other.

Your relationship with loved ones may go through different stages when you return home. Things might start out great (the "honeymoon" stage) but get harder as you spend more time together. This is a common experience, and you're not alone.

## Four Common Relationship Stages During Reentry

| Stage 1: Honeymoon. | Stage 2: Uncertainty and suspicion. | Stage 3: Testing and learning to share. | Stage 4: Belonging. |
|---|---|---|---|
| You and your loved ones are excited to be back together. Everyone's at their best, but anxiety is under the surface. | You and your loved ones might feel uncertain about your relationship and question motives. Are you going to stick around? Do you still want to be together? | You and your loved ones may test each other to see if it's OK to share feelings and be yourself. Can you trust each other? | You may struggle with how to get involved in family routines, but success at this stage can lead to stability. What roles will you play? How can you be part of family life again? |

You don't have to face relationship challenges alone! You can go here for help:

- **Family-oriented reentry programs.** Phalanx Family Services, based in Chicago, is an example of such a program. They help people reunite with their families after prison. Learn more at www.phalanxgrpservices.org . Look for similar programs in your community.
- **Classes.** Anger management, parenting, communication, or marriage and family classes can help you develop skills that will make your relationships stronger.
- **Counseling or therapy**, either alone or with your partner or family. See the Trauma and Mental Health chapter for more information (on p. 68).
- **Returning-resident support groups.** Many community organizations offer supportive circles where you can share your struggles with others who share a similar background. Local reentry organizations may be able to connect you with these groups for advice and support.
- If you are in an abusive relationship, **call the National Domestic Violence Hotline:** 1-800-799-SAFE (7233).

There is no "one-size-fits-all" solution to the challenges people face when reuniting with loved ones. Below, formerly incarcerated people share their advice about reconnecting with loved ones. This chapter covers the following topics:

- Self-Advocacy
- Sharing (Self-Disclosure)
- Parenting After Release
- Dealing with Difficult Emotions
- Anger Management
- Institutionalization
- Domestic Violence

## Self-Advocacy

Self-advocacy is the ability to speak up for yourself. It's being able to identify your needs, communicate them clearly, and help others understand how they can support you. People who have been in prison often have to work on this skill. When you stood up for yourself in prison, it may have led to fights or disciplinary consequences. Many formerly incarcerated people try to avoid conflict because they want to avoid violence. Or they have trouble communicating their needs calmly and kindly. The first step to developing healthy self-advocacy skills is to recognize that this may be a challenge for you. Practice expressing your needs in low-stakes situations with people you trust who want to see you succeed. Then you'll be better at speaking up for yourself in all situations.

*Learn to set boundaries.*

—**Erick N.**

## Sharing (Self-Disclosure)

Many people survive prison by becoming closed off and guarded. They seldom share things with others. But being closed off can hurt your relationships. Family members can also become closed off. They might only share positive things during their visits, or visit rarely because it's too painful.

Tony explains why many people in prison are closed off from their family:

*You keep [your family] at an arm's length because you know you could lose them. A lot of us watched family members die. Family members get sick. Family members move away. You're watching the world go past you, and to keep that family interested in your life and to keep yourself interested in their life is really hard because you can't experience that life with them.*

As Pablo warns, isolation helps people cope in prison, but it's not always helpful on the outside.

*The coping mechanisms we had on the inside are still with us, and they create barriers on the outside. When you retract and people are not knowing the reason for your isolation, they think it's having to do with them.*

So how do you open up when you're used to being closed off? How do you learn to share?

**Self-disclosure** is sharing meaningful information about ourselves. It is being honest with your loved ones. It is one of the most important parts of a healthy relationship. It

- builds trust,
- provides emotional release, and
- encourages your loved ones to share, too.

There are risks to sharing. You may worry that your loved ones will reject you if they know how you feel. You may worry that you will hurt others if you share what you have experienced. You may feel embarrassed to admit that you need help. You may feel that your family members won't be able to understand what you have gone through. All this can make you want to hold back.

Keep in mind that closeness doesn't happen overnight. You can choose what to share and when.

When building relationships, most people share slowly. They take small steps and wait to see how people respond. Here are some tips for learning to open up to loved ones again:

- **Start with the easy stuff.** Share what you like to do for fun. Ask them what they like to do. What movies do they love? What do they do to relax?
- **Spend time together.** Take long walks. As you do, share some of your feelings, fears, and goals. Invite them to open up, too. Start small and see how they respond.
- **Share over text.** Send short, friendly messages about your day to your family and friends. Ask how they are doing.
- **Avoid criticizing or offering advice** when your loved ones share with you. Just listen. Be positive and supportive.
- **Be willing to talk about your relationship.** How has your relationship changed? How can you perform your share of the work?

Keke describes the small ways he shares his life with his children and invites them to share their lives with him:

> *I take time out of my day, even five minutes, to call them and see what's going on. I text them every day, every morning.... I talk to them and get their point of view and see what's going on, try to spend time. I tell them I love them, how you are doing, how your day is going, what you got planned. Little simple stuff. I let them talk.*

David notes that if you want your children to open up to you, it helps to not be critical:

> *In prison I became more educated, more aware. My relationships with my children became complicated because I had the tendency to correct them in their behavior. I was bombarding them with advice, and the more I did this, the more they were pushing me away. I had to learn to relax, to not be overbearing.*

Pablo also notes the importance of listening:

> *Be ready to hear some truths. Listen attentively. There is a lot of lived life in your absence. Everybody was in a bad situation. As we were surviving, so were they. Don't approach it with judgment. Try to be understanding with your family and with yourself.*

Keke notes the importance of being open and honest with your partner:

> *The most challenging thing is [to] be honest with [your partner]. If she's taking time out of her life to stand by you, give her your life. [Don't] feed her a fairy tale.... Don't come out trying to feed nobody no dream and definitely don't feed yourself a dream.*

## Sharing Your Past with Others

If you are in the habit of closing yourself off, it can be hard to make new friends. There are a few methods for doing so below, and you can choose what you think would work best for you. Tony explains:

> *You spend so much time keeping people at arm's distance. You never let anybody get close. [When you go into prison,] you're so young, you're so vibrant, it's so easy to have friends, to have relationships, to have people that are close to you. But when you come home, you've gotten so used to keeping people at a distance that you just continue to do it. It's hard to make new friends.*

When meeting new people, it can be hard to know how much to share about your past. Not everyone will be accepting of who you are. Roberto talks about the challenge of getting to know people and deciding how much to share:

> *How do I get to know people? How do you create a personal brand so that all the good things you offer are not eclipsed by the fact that you spent a significant amount of time in prison? How do you open a conversation with someone when you're trying to remain private, and also take into account all of the negative stigma that's attached to being incarcerated? You're just meeting people and you don't want to share too much about yourself. There's so much negative stigma. You have to break through that wall. On the other hand, if you do, it's still no guarantee that they are going to relate to you and understand what you're going through.*

Keke prefers telling people right away about his past. "I tell them in the door," he says. He continues:

> *I learned from my experience that if you lay your cards out in the open, you get a better understanding. Nowadays, people Google so*

*much. Both of you have to be honest with each other. So that's what I do. I let them know right in the door. This is me. I've been to prison twice. I'm doing this, I'm doing that, trying to get myself together.*

Tony also prefers being open:

*It's a little weird, a little awkward, to just come out and say, hey, I just spent ten years in prison. But I've never been one to be shy. I've always been real open about what I went through because it lets other people know that, look, just because I was in there doesn't mean I have to keep going back and forth, back and forth.*

Heather, on the other hand, is more reserved:

*I don't really mention [that I was in prison] to people. But, I guess it helps to have moved away to a different state, so really not that many people know me. They just know what they see of me now. They don't know ... I made mistakes in the past. And I'm kind of comfortable with it. So, if I was to meet a guy or something and start dating, I wouldn't just throw all my dirty laundry out front. I'd get to know him. But if things were working out really good, I'd tell him all about it, and if he didn't accept it, then he probably wouldn't be the guy for me anyway.*

Tony concludes, "When you meet somebody, if it scares them that you've been to prison, then you know what? That's not the person that you need to be with."

When you are deciding how to share your past with people, consider these guidelines:

1. Is the other person important to you? If so, sharing may help you be closer.
2. What is the risk of sharing your past with them? Could they tell others or make it more difficult for you to get a job? Could they use it against you in other ways?
3. Is it appropriate to share? Sometimes it's wise to not share too much with strangers. What do they need to know about your past?
4. Will the other person be willing to share, too? Good relationships are built on reciprocity (a willingness to share on both sides).
5. Is sharing going to help or hurt? Think about the effect your sharing will have on the other person.

# Asking for Help and Setting Boundaries

If you're used to being closed off, it may be especially hard to ask for help from loved ones. Pablo notes:

*My family thinks that because I'm free, all my problems are over, but I need assistance with the most basic things. That does make me somewhat defensive, and I'll end up trying to do things on my own and then I crash and burn.*

His advice? "Ditch that machismo and ask for help. It's not a bad thing."

It can be embarrassing to have to ask for help. As Joe Joe explains:

*What we're competing with is not [wanting to feel] like a helpless infant all the time. We're so used to being rejected that we don't reach out much for help.*

Lee, whose partner was incarcerated, says that "healthy adult relationships aren't about putting your needs in the back seat." She explains:

*You want to be considerate and not wear out your welcome. The effect of that is that maybe you're not expressing the things that you need. It's OK to say, "Hey, I need you to do this thing for me." Learn to communicate what you need.*

Joe Joe offers this final piece of advice regarding asking for help:

*If you strive to lighten someone's load rather than adding to it, they are going to be more receptive to helping you. This is what really wins people over and will help get you where you need to go.*

Some people going through reentry struggle to set boundaries with their loved ones. Your loved ones are happy to have you back. They may pressure you to get involved or do things you aren't ready for yet.

They may ask you to do too many things at once. It's OK to step back and take things slow. It's OK to say no to things and let them know that you aren't ready yet.

*You have to take things slow. All these new experiences, it can be extremely overwhelming. All those people tugging at you—those are extra stressors. Listen, take care of yourself.*

—**Ricky**

*I love a good challenge. I was pulled into a monkey bar contest, into diving off the high board. But these old bones are not the same as they were. You don't want to injure yourself.*

—**Kilroy**

*We're coming out feeling beholden to people for what they've done for us while we're inside, or for our loved ones. That clouds our judgment, our best interest. Realize you can't help anybody if you're not helping yourself. Being selfish is not a bad thing. If love is directed inwards, it can radiate outwards. You can't help anybody if you're not helping yourself.*

—**Pablo**

# Parenting After Release

If you are a parent, you may be nervous about reuniting with your kids. You may feel guilt for what your kids have gone through while you were locked up. Some parents need or want time to get their feet on the ground before getting their kids back. These feelings are normal.

Lots of people have unrealistic expectations of parents, especially of mothers. You may feel pressure to make up for lost time with your kids, to be a super parent, or to spend lots of time and money on your kids. "Super parents" are expected to always be there emotionally for their kids, and always place the needs of their children above their own. They are expected to have a clean house and money to put their kids in good programs. Parents who cannot or do not meet this ideal are often seen as bad.

**These "super parent" ideals are impossible to live up to. And that's OK. Resist the urge to parent out of guilt.**

Don't be too hard on yourself. You are going to make mistakes. We all do. Take mistakes as an opportunity to learn. Be willing to learn from your children, too. Building a healthy relationship with your children will take hard work, love, and compassion. It will take time and patience, but it is worth it.

Some relationships may never entirely heal. Accept that your children and loved ones may not want the same kind of relationship you once had.

Here are a few things you can do to make reunifying with your family easier:

- **Educate yourself.** Read books and attend classes about parenting. Raising a child is always hard, so get all the tools you can.
- **Get counseling or therapy.** It can help you heal and provide tools for you to be a better parent. See the Trauma and Mental Health chapter (on p. 68).

- **Do things you enjoy. Meditate.** Take some time to do things for yourself if you can. See the Mindfulness chapter (on p. 126).

- **Talk to other parents,** especially those who have spent time in prison. Join a moms group, a dads group, or a parents group. Share your experiences, fears, and dreams.

*Always remember that reconciliation and restoration are two different things. You may reconcile, but the relationship may never be restored. Just grieve properly. Be OK with that. Don't walk around forever with the grief on your back. If you've done all you can, it will be OK.*

—**Josephine**

*There will be people in your life who will remain after such a long journey, and there will be some that fall to the wayside. Don't look back. Keep looking forward, looking inward. Seek inward happiness.*

—**Pablo**

 ## Reflect

1. What feelings do you have about reuniting with your kids?

2. How can you practice self-care during this time?

3. Where can you go for help? Who is in your support network?

> *You can't recapture time that has been lost. You have to start fresh. Don't be too gung-ho. Trust has to be reestablished. If they're angry, don't try to invalidate their anger. Talk about it. Don't pretend that the separation never happened, because it did. Try to seek counseling.*
>
> **—Josephine**

> *When you're locked up, you have all this time to sit and think. You have ideas of how you want things to go, and then you get out and, of course, those are just ideas. . . . Take care of yourself and everything else will fall into place. . . . You can't stress out over everything that you have no control over. Don't give up hope. There's always hope. And love overcomes a lot of stuff.*
>
> **—Heather**

# Dealing with Difficult Emotions

In prison, you may have bottled up difficult emotions instead of working through them. Maybe you pushed aside feelings of fear, guilt, or anger and instead told family members that everything was going to be OK. Your family members may have done the same.

Here are a few of the emotions you might feel as you reunite with your loved ones:

- **Fear** is your body's reaction to danger or uncertainty. You may fear that nobody will love you because of the things you've done. You may be afraid that your children won't accept you. This fear can cause you to withdraw from them even more.
- **Sadness** is feeling unhappy or discouraged. You might feel discouraged that your children don't know you or that your sister doesn't want to talk to you.
- **Grief** is a profound feeling of loss. You might feel a sense of loss for the years you spent in prison, away from your family.
- **Guilt** is feeling bad about yourself, often for something you've done or haven't done that made others suffer. You might feel guilty for not being around for your family.
- **Anger** is something you feel when someone or something has done you wrong. You might feel angry about what prison has done to you, or angry about something a loved one has said.

People experience emotions through their mind and body. For instance, fear can tighten your chest. You might feel sick to your stomach or start sweating. Some emotions can help you change and grow. Others can keep you from growing and harm your relationships.

Expect some of your repressed emotions to surface. Sounds, tastes, and smells can trigger memories from the past. You've lost partners, friends, and parents. Expect to feel rage, sorrow, frustration, and grief.

*If you have any emotions at all, you're going to have guilt about making your family suffer… They suffer with you while you're in there. To them, you're kind of dead because you're not around any longer. There is guilt. And we don't like to show it because, hey, we're tough guys.*

**—Tony**

*I was looking at videos with a friend and a song came on. I found myself crying for no apparent reason. I lost my father when I was locked up. That was one of his favorite songs. I had never had the opportunity to mourn. All of the pain came forward.*

**—Pablo**

It's normal to feel these emotions. It's what you do with these emotions that matters. Pushing aside difficult emotions instead of feeling and understanding them can harm your relationships. Learning to recognize, express, and manage emotions can help you have healthier relationships.

Here are some tips for managing emotions in healthier ways:

- **Identify your feelings. Let them wash over you.** They won't last forever. Give yourself time to feel them. Don't bury them. Doing so can cause these feelings to build up even more.
- **Recognize the difference between feeling and acting.** Just because you feel a certain way doesn't mean you have to act on it.
- **Accept responsibility for your feelings.** Try not to blame others for the way you feel. Instead of saying, "You're making me angry," say "I'm feeling angry."
- **Express your feelings in helpful ways.** Separate people from their actions. "I'm angry about something you have done," not "I am angry with you."
- **Change your perception.** Think about what caused you to feel that way. Are there different ways to think about what happened that are more helpful?

Therapists or counselors can help you work through and manage your emotions. It may help to go to family or couples' therapy. Some organizations offer support for families working through the challenges of reentry. Ask to be connected to these resources at a local reentry organization (see the directory on p. 135).

In prison, you may have walked away from difficult emotions and conflicts. Perhaps you had space to think through difficult issues before facing them. On the outside, you may be expected to directly address issues with your loved ones rather than walking away. You may feel pressure to respond right away when you'd rather take your time.

Pablo explains what happens when you retreat instead of talking about how you are feeling with loved ones:

> *When you retreat, it telegraphs to the other person that you don't care. When you remain silent, people may think you're brushing them off.*

It's OK to take some time to think before talking through a problem. As Lee explains, "It's OK to say, 'I need time to think about this, I can't give you an answer right away.'"

But too often when people retreat, they never come back to it. If you need some space, commit to talking about it later.

# Anger Management

As with other emotions, it's normal to feel and express anger. It gets to be a problem if it is out of control, aggressive, or constant. It's a problem if it hurts the people around you.

Anger is a secondary emotion. For example, "He embarrassed me, then I got angry." Getting to the root of why you were embarrassed can help the anger subside.

You may have to take an anger management class as a condition of your parole. These classes can help you learn some basic skills for managing your anger. A therapist or counselor can also help. Anger management classes or therapy may cover topics such as:

- Causes and triggers of your anger
- Better ways to express your anger
- Taking time out for reflection
- Understanding the effects of your anger

**Need to find an anger management class?** If it's required for parole, you will need to make sure that it offers a certificate. Often there is a small fee for this certificate. Ask questions to make sure. You can usually take the class online or in person.

To find a low or no-cost anger management class, try the following resources:

- The National Domestic Violence Hotline, 1-800-799-SAFE (7233)
- Emotions Anonymous, a national 12-step program with virtual and in-person meetings: emotionsanonymous.org
- The National Anger Management Association's national directory of certified anger-management specialists: nama.memberclicks.net
- Ask your parole officer or healthcare provider for suggestions.
- Community centers and local universities, colleges, and nonprofits sometimes offer anger management classes for the public.
- Search for anger management classes and community resources at your states' department of human services' website.

Here are some anger management tips, modified from experts at the Mayo Clinic:

| Tactic | Insight |
|---|---|
| Think before you speak. | In the heat of the moment, it's easy to say something you'll later regret. Take a few moments to collect your thoughts. Allow others to do the same. |
| Once you're calm, express your anger. | As soon as you're thinking clearly, express your anger, concerns, and needs clearly and directly. Do so without trying to hurt or control others. |
| Get some exercise. | Exercise can help reduce stress that can cause you to become angry. If you feel your anger building, go for a run. |
| Take a timeout. | Give yourself a short break when things get stressful. A few moments of quiet time might help you handle things better. |
| Identify possible solutions. | Instead of focusing on what made you mad, work on resolving the issue. Does your child's messy room stress you out? Close the door. Is your partner late for dinner every night? Schedule meals later in the evening—or agree to eat on your own sometimes. |
| Stick with 'I' statements. | To avoid placing blame, use "I" statements. Be respectful and specific. For example, say, "I'm upset that you left the table without asking to help with the dishes" instead of "You never do any housework." |
| Use humor to release tension. | Humor can help you face what's making you angry without getting out of control. |
| Relax. | When your temper flares, put relaxation skills to work. Take deep breaths. Imagine a calm place or repeat a calming phrase, such as "Take it easy." Listen to music or go for a walk. Practice mindfulness (see the Mindfulness chapter on p. 126). |
| Know when to seek help. | Learning to control anger is hard for everyone at times. Seek help if your anger seems out of control, causes you to do things you regret, or hurts those around you. |

 # Reflect

1. Think about a time when you felt angry and it got out of control. What happened? Why did it get out of control?

2. Now think about how you could have managed your anger better. What are some things you can try next time you get angry?

..........................................................................

# Institutionalization

Many people who have left prison continue to suffer the mental effects of being locked up long after they leave. Institutionalization is how your thoughts, speech, and actions are influenced by being locked up. You and your loved ones may not be aware of the many ways prison has impacted you. This can cause all sorts of conflicts and misunderstandings.

Some people who leave prison suffer from Post-Incarceration Syndrome (PIS), a syndrome similar to Post-Traumatic Stress Syndrome (PTSD). Time in prison can make mental health problems worse. It can make people more isolated and more violent. It can lead some people to feel that they have no purpose. It can make people fearful and hyper-vigilant.

Here are just a few of the many ways that time in prison may have impacted you and your relationships:

- *I closed myself off as a way of coping.* —**Anonymous**
- *I have these defense mechanisms. I've learned to telegraph assertiveness and square up when faced with conflict.* —**Pablo**
- *I had hangups about talking to regular, free people. I didn't feel comfortable.* —**Ricky**
- *When I get upset, my posture says I'm ready for a fight.* —**Pablo**
- *In prison, we got up early. I'm up in the middle of the night. Up early in the morning.* —**Anonymous**
- *In prison, you have to watch your back. Now on the outside, I can't sit with my back to people. I have to be at the back of the room so I can see everyone.* —**Kilroy**
- *I'm loud because in jail, people tend to scream. Everyone has to speak over each other if they want to be heard.* —**Antonio**

The tools you used to survive in prison were "blunt tools," as Pablo describes. You may have survived by being closed off, aggressive, and hypervigilant, or by being loud and watching your back. On the outside, these tactics can drive away your loved ones.

You will need to add new tools to your toolbox—tools that are more gentle and precise. They include listening, communicating, and being patient with each other. Have honest talks with loved ones. Invite them to help you recognize when you are acting in an aggressive way. Practice adjusting your body language.

It will take time for you and your loved ones to understand just how much your time in prison has impacted you. You may need counseling or help from a support group to work through these issues.

Mapping Your Future, National Edition

# Domestic Violence

Domestic violence isn't just an anger problem. It's about control. Domestic violence is defined as violent or aggressive behavior within the home, typically involving the violent abuse of a spouse or partner.

It can take many forms, including:
- Verbal abuse (threats, name-calling, intimidation)
- Physical abuse (pushing, slapping, choking)
- Controlling behavior (destroying property; keeping you from seeing people, going places, or spending money)
- Emotional abuse (making you feel like you are worthless)
- Sexual abuse (unwanted sexual activity, often using force)

In some families or cultures, these behaviors are not seen as wrong. It's hard to break away from domestic violence when the attitudes about relationships around you are not healthy. It may take some time to change your way of thinking. It may take some time to realize that what you are doing or experiencing is wrong.

If you are in an abusive relationship, seek help. Making the decision to leave is hard. It can be risky. It takes courage to leave, especially if you fear for your own safety or the safety of your children. It's hard to leave if you depend on the other person for money.

Begin by calling the National Domestic Violence hotline: 1-800-799-SAFE (7233). This **confidential**, free 24-hour hotline provides support, information, and referrals. It can put you in touch with resources in your area. Even if you are not ready to leave the relationship, the hotline can help you get through hard times. It can help you take the next step.

Additional resources for survivors of domestic violence can be found at ncadv.org/resources .

For a list of places where you can go for help in your community do a search at www.domesticshelters.org/help .

If money is keeping you from leaving a partner who is abusing you, there may be an emergency crisis fund for survivors of domestic violence in your community. Search online for "domestic violence support," "crisis fund," and the name of your city, town, or county.

We have listed transitional housing and emergency shelter options in the directories at the end of this book (see p. 135). Many of these shelters serve people who are leaving an abusive relationship. Some provide protection if you fear for your safety. The directories also list counseling resources available to people who are facing domestic violence.

## If You are the Abusive Partner

If you have been abusive to a partner or family member, reach out to get help. The first important step is to acknowledge you have a problem. You can change, but it will take work. You may be required to stay away from your partner until you are in a better place, or you may choose to stay away for a while to keep them safe and give them some space.

To get help, consider attending a program for those who have been abusive. Programs like these will help you
- see that it is NOT ok to abuse a partner,
- learn to take blame and credit for your actions, and
- learn nonviolent and non-controlling ways to communicate and behave.

These programs vary by state, but you can search online locally for keywords like "domestic abuse intervention." For more information about what to expect with these programs, visit www.thehotline.org/resources/intervention-programs-for-abusive-behavior .

In Illinois, you could enroll in the Partner Abuse Intervention Program (PAIP), for people who control their partners with physical abuse, emotional abuse, sexual abuse, or economic abuse (withholding money). In Minnesota, the Duluth Model helps people who want to change abusive behavior: www.theduluthmodel.org . Search for similar programs in your state.

 # Reflect

1. What does a healthy relationship look like to you?

2. Think back on your relationships with your family or loved ones. In what ways were they healthy? In what ways were they unhealthy?

3. Where are the places you can go for help if you are in an abusive relationship?

*You always have to see the silver lining in the clouds, no matter how murky they are. I think that's the main advice that I could give to someone. Just don't give up. Because it's hard. Don't make no mistake about it.*

**—Anonymous**

# Mindfulness

Mindfulness can help you deal with the stress of reentry. This chapter covers the following topics:

- What Is Mindfulness?
- What Are the Benefits of Mindfulness?
- How Do I Meditate?
- Meditation Scripts
- Mindfulness Resources
- Meditation Groups

## What Is Mindfulness?

Mindfulness is about paying attention to the present. It is about noticing your thoughts, emotions, and how your body feels. It's about not judging yourself or giving yourself a hard time. When you are aware of your five senses and your mind, you are being mindful!

Mindfulness is not about fixing what is wrong with you. Instead, it is about accepting what is going on inside you. It's about being gentle and kind to yourself. It helps us stay connected to the moment. We can then respond in healthy, caring ways.

Mindfulness has its roots in Buddhism, but mindfulness is not a religion. Instead, it is a way to explore your mind and body. Some people see mindfulness in every religion. Prayer can be a form of mindfulness.

*Does your heart race every time you step out of your house or enter a public place? Practicing mindfulness helped me be aware of physically overwhelming experiences at the onset. I could feel perspiration on my upper lip. My palms start getting sweaty. My body tenses up. These are the warning signs that remind me to just breathe. During these episodes, I found that I was not breathing. Doing nothing else but concentrating on my breathing made this experience bearable. Soon thereafter, I was more and more in control.*

**—Mindfulness program participant**

# What Are the Benefits of Mindfulness?

Mindfulness has many benefits. It can help you manage stress and control your emotions. It can help you not get stuck in bad thoughts. It can help you be happier. It can even change how your brain works. Other benefits include:

- Better ability to fight disease
- Lower blood pressure and heart rate
- Better mental focus
- Better handling of emotions
- Lower anxiety and depression
- More growth after trauma
- More self-compassion
- Less burnout

*Have you felt alone, out of place? You are not alone. I experience that regularly. No one seems to understand what I am experiencing. I rely on mindfulness to assist me in channeling my focus. I do so by simply concentrating on the breath. This simple act is what grounds me and allows me to function normally.*

**—Anonymous**

# How Do I Meditate?

Meditation is a common way to practice mindfulness.

**No training is needed to meditate!** There is no one right way to meditate. There is no "good" way, and certainly no "bad" way. If you can breathe, you can meditate.

**Practice alone or with a group.** You can meditate alone or with a group, or you could find someone who knows how to meditate to help you get started.

**When to practice.** In the beginning, try to meditate for 5 or 10 minutes. Make that time longer bit by bit. Try different times of the day: morning, evening, or afternoon. Try to practice every day. But, if something comes up, that's OK! Let go of what you think should happen, but return to your practice when you can.

**How to sit.** Many people meditate sitting down with their eyes closed or open. Sit in a chair or cross-legged on a pillow, floor, or bed. Sit up straight, but be relaxed. Rest your hands in your lap or on your legs.

**Common difficulties.** It's normal to feel restless, bored, and sleepy. Your mind may wander. That's totally okay. You don't need to get rid of thoughts when you are meditating. Do your best to notice your thoughts. Label them as they come. You might label them things like "thinking about the past," "restless," or "bored." Then, see if you can bring your attention to your breathing. Meditation takes practice. Do your best to be curious. No matter what happens, try not to judge yourself. And when you do judge yourself, just notice it (maybe say "judging" to yourself), and then go back to your breath.

**Meditation and trauma.** Sometimes meditation makes you remember things. It may dig up traumatic memories. This may make you feel stressed or anxious. Meditation can help you deal with these feelings. But, it is not a cure-all. If focusing on your body brings up traumatic memories, try focusing on a safe image or sound. If difficult memories keep coming, talk with a mental health professional. Look for a meditation group for people who have trauma.

# Meditation Scripts

Many people use a script for meditation. A meditation script is a set of words you can read or listen to while meditating. Read each script slowly to get used to it. After a while, you can say the words silently to yourself. Give each step about 1 minute, but feel free to go at your own pace.

*I don't always follow a specific regimen other than just to breathe in times of stress. This sounds simple enough but it can be very difficult, especially when you are not practicing regularly.*

**—Anonymous**

### A Seated Breath and Body Meditation Practice | Abbreviated from Mindful Magazine

1. Begin by getting comfortable, sitting up straight but not rigid, in a position of ease. Close your eyes or lower your gaze toward the floor.
2. Take a few deep breaths. Get a sense of how you're doing at this moment physically, emotionally, and mentally. Is there tension or tightness anywhere? Is your mind busy or calm?
3. As you breathe in, bring a beginner's mind, noticing things for the first time. As you breathe out, bring the same sense. Rest your awareness on the breath.
4. Begin to sense your body sitting here. Feel into your whole body. What are your senses telling you? You may feel warm or cold. You may be itchy. Perhaps some areas don't have any feeling at all – a blank. Spend the next minute feeling these sensations. Allow them to come and go.
5. If your mind wanders, where is it wandering to? Are you remembering something? Are you feeling anger or regret? Are you practicing what you will say to someone? Notice your thoughts as if you were sitting in a movie theater, watching images come and go on the screen. Notice the thought or emotion as if it were someone else's thought, not yours. Notice an opening up in yourself as you become more aware, more accepting.
6. Come back to the breath. Breathe in and out. Notice how the whole body expands when you inhale, and contracts when you exhale. The whole body is breathing.
7. As you end, congratulate yourself for taking time to meditate. Notice if you feel any different than you did when you began. Realize that you can take a few minutes to meditate whenever you wish.

*Have you experienced disappointment? I have and that is not something to be ashamed of. I constantly ruminate on these disappointments. Rumination occurs naturally when you allow your mind to take control. Mindfulness has taught me how to take control of my thought process. This has allowed me the freedom to take life as it comes and adjust as needed.*

**—Mindfulness program participant**

*Gratitude Meditations*

A gratitude practice can help us tap into hope. It can help us boost our mood and keep going when things are hard. Try this basic gratitude meditation (adapted from JoAnna Hardy's Morning Gratitude meditation on the 10 Percent Happier app). Give it 5 to 15 minutes. If it helps you, return to it when you need a lift, or use it as your daily practice:

1. Take some time to get comfortable. Sit or stand, with your back upright but relaxed. Take a few deep breaths. Let your chest rise and your belly fill with each breath. Each time you exhale, let go of any tension in your face, your shoulders, your neck, your belly, your legs.
2. When you feel ready, let your eyes drift closed or downward and your breathing return to normal. Gently rest your attention on your breath. Stay here for a little while, allowing thoughts to come and go like clouds through an open sky. Each time you become distracted, let your attention return to your breath.
3. After your mind has calmed, one at a time, focus on three things you are grateful for, each one in the here-and-now: You woke up this morning. You can breathe fresh air to fill your lungs. Your heart is sending oxygen to your fingertips. You can feel the air all around you. Keep this simple, happy, and in the present.
4. Next, think of three things that you are grateful for that will happen in the next hour: Making your breakfast, seeing a familiar face, the smell or taste of your coffee. Stay with each one, think about their goodness, and focus on how it feels to feel grateful for these things. Where in your body do you feel gratefulness? How do you recognize that feeling?
5. Finally, think of three bigger things that you're grateful for: a pet or loved one, someone who loves you or has shown you love, or perhaps a community or even a job or a thing that brings you happiness. If you become distracted, let your attention return to your breath, and then return to these things you feel grateful for in the world around you.
6. Focus again on the feeling of gratitude, if you have it. If you don't, that's OK. Sometimes we don't feel gratitude. If you do feel it, where in your body does it live? How does it feel? Stay here for a little while and feel the gratitude in your body as you continue to breathe. Allow this feeling to warm and fill you with each inhale. Know that you can draw on this feeling as a source of strength and resilience in the rest of your life.
7. After some time here, release your focus and relax. Open your eyes. Notice if you feel any different now than you did when you began this meditation.

Here's a second gratitude meditation (adapted from Mindvalley Institute) specifically aimed at helping you change an attitude that's working against you. It's not easy to focus on the positive when you feel stressed, so be patient with yourself as you try this meditation. You can always return to the breath, if it feels too stressful.

1. As you did above, sit in a comfortable position. Take a few deep and slow breaths.
2. Think about something that's troubling you. It's best to start small. Name something that annoys you. Perhaps the room you're in is cold and drafty.
3. Now see if you can flip it to something positive. For example, perhaps the room is cold and drafty, but it's raining and you're able to stay dry.
4. Continue to think of things or experiences that you don't like. Do your best to find something positive about each thing or experience. Challenge yourself. Maybe they are helping you learn or grow. Perhaps you notice how you have kept going even when things are hard. Maybe you have found new ideas you didn't have before.
5. You can also simply repeat, "I am grateful for _____" and notice what comes up.

*Mindful Walking | Adapted from Mindful Walking, Segal, Williams, and Teasdale Mindfulness-Based Cognitive Therapy for Depression*

Mindfulness is about being aware of what you're doing, thinking, and feeling. Walking mindfulness is simple. You can do it without people knowing what you're doing. Everybody walks, but most of us don't focus on the process of walking and how the body feels.

1. Standing still, become aware of your feet. How do your feet feel when they touch the ground? Bend your knees a few times to get a sense of how your feet and legs feel.
2. When you start walking, notice how you move your weight into each leg. One leg "empties" and the other leg takes over to support your body.
3. With one leg "empty," allow the other heel to rise slowly. Move it forward, feeling your leg. Place it down to get ready for the next step. Feel your weight move to this leg.
4. Continue walking. Notice how your feet, legs, hips, and upper body feel.
5. If you stop, notice how you feel when you stand. Notice how it feels when you start moving again.

> *Remind yourself that the deepest stillness and peace does not arise because the world is still or the mind is quiet. Stillness is nourished when we allow the world, the mind, and the body to be just as they are for now, moment by moment, and breath by breath.*
>
> —**Williams & Penman**, *Mindfulness: A Practical Guide to Finding Peace in a Frantic World*

# Meditation Resources

Need more meditations? Check out this website for more meditation scripts: tinyurl.com/MDG-Meditation-Scripts .

If you would like to learn about meditation from people of color, check out this resource guide: tinyurl.com/ejp-BIPOC-mindfulness .

**Phone apps.** There are lots of free mindfulness phone apps. These apps offer guided meditations, timers, calming sounds, soothing voices, tips, and more. Some provide tips on how to sleep better or be less anxious.

These phone apps can be used on the bus or train, at work, or before bed. You can choose long or short meditations. Want to learn how to download a Phone App? Go to the Technology chapter (see p. 86).

# Meditation Groups

Meditation groups are a great way to meet people and practice. If you are a beginner, they can help you learn. They can help you keep going when you feel like quitting. Some are face-to-face while others are online. Many groups begin with a few friends meeting in someone's home.

Some meditation groups may say they are Buddhist. They may use words like "Sangha" (community), "Zen" (meditative state), or "Vipassana" (insight). You may not have to be Buddhist to join. Many groups are open to anyone joining their group.

You may be able to find a mental health mindfulness group. These groups are more structured. Here are two mental health mindfulness programs that may be helpful:

- Mindfulness Based Stress Reduction (MBSR) is an eight-week-long group program offered by meditation and wellness centers and many hospitals across the country. It helps people develop the skills to deal with chronic pain and cope with stress of all kinds. Search for "MBSR near me" to find local programs.

- Mindfulness Based Cognitive Therapy (MBCT) is like MBSR, but with more focus on the skills needed to deal with anxiety and depression. It explores patterns of thinking and helps people shift to more helpful attitudes. Search for "MBCT near me" to find local programs.

*It is common to question your purpose. I do so repeatedly. My relationships aren't exactly as I had envisioned. Mindfulness meditation provided me the space and compassion to accept people as they come. I learned to let the little things go and focus on what makes that person special to me.*

**—Mindfulness program participant**

# Connecting With Your Community

After being released from prison, many people find it hard to connect with others. You were separated from your family and friends. Now you may feel loneliness and isolation, especially if the people you were close to are no longer around.

Getting involved in your community and making new friends might help you begin to heal. This may mean working to make a difference through politics, organizing, and volunteering. This may mean writing letters to elected officials, campaigning, voting, participating in government events, and talking to people in your community.

## Community Organizing and Advocacy

A community can be people who live in the same area, or people who have something in common. Community organizing is when community members join together and push for their needs and rights. Community organizing is a tool for making your voice heard and creating positive change. You would be surprised by what you can do when you join together with others to make sure your community's voice is being heard.

Community organizing can include:
- Gathering information about your community's needs
- Going door-to-door to share information
- Giving public speeches
- Setting up meetings
- Sharing information about your community with the public
- Developing community leadership
- Coordinating fundraisers

There are many organizations that do community organizing online and on the ground. Now that you are out of prison, you can help them in important ways. You can help change the laws that affect people who have been in prison. The best place to start is by hooking up with the organizations already doing good work in your community.

To find how you can get more involved in your community, talk to people at your local reentry organization. If that doesn't work, try some of the suggestions in the next section. Each one is aimed at setting you up to become more active in your community.

*Get involved in advocacy work. If we want to change the process, we have to lead the process.*

—**Marlon C.**

# Getting Involved in Your Community

Find local organizations, community activities, and ways to get involved at these community centers or with these services:

**Religious Organizations.** Churches, synagogues, mosques, or other religious communities can help you find meaning, purpose, and fellowship. Many religious organizations have classes, support groups, and volunteer opportunities. Don't worry if it takes a while for you to find the place that feels right for you.

**Libraries.** Public libraries organize events and classes. They have book clubs, social gatherings, and concerts. Many also have a space where people can post information about community events, group meetings, and even job openings. Visit your local library's website or stop by in-person to see what's happening in your community.

**Reentry Programs.** If you live in a town with a reentry program, consider volunteering your time there. Even if you didn't use this program, you could help people who are getting out now. Let them know you are happy to help. With some luck, you may even be able to turn your volunteer work into a paid job. You can start your search for local programs with the resources in the directory (see p. 135).

**City and County Park Districts and Forest Preserves.** Your town or city probably has a park district, and its website will include information about the parks in your area. Take time to visit these parks and spend time in nature. Many park districts offer sports programs and leagues, as well as other recreational programs.

**Free City Papers.** In many cities you can get free alternative papers weekly (like the Anchorage Press in Alaska or the Village Voice in New York). They usually have local reporting on community issues and information on concerts, local events, and classes. The same information should also be on the paper's website.

*Don't give up. Do what you can to promote change. Take the time out to try to mentor some of these young people that are out here in the hopes that, one day, we can bring about changes. Instead of wondering when somebody else is gonna do something about it, I need to remember that I'm somebody and try to do what I can.*

**–Anonymous**

# Serving Your Community

Volunteer work gives you the chance to make friends, solve problems, and do some good for your community. It is also good for your health. Making new friends can prevent feelings of sadness and make you feel less alone. Watching your community improve—through the work that you've done—can give you a sense of pride and fulfillment.

If you are out of work, volunteering can also help you get new skills to add to your resume. You may also meet new people who can help you network and find new job opportunities. Volunteering expands your life in ways that may surprise you. You may discover new abilities or find new interests.

Some places you can volunteer are:

- Senior living centers and nursing homes
- Humane societies
- Homeless shelters
- Food banks
- Local places of worship

Call or visit to ask how you can help out. You can also do a Google search for volunteer opportunities in your community.

Mapping Your Future, National Edition

# Part 4: Directory

- National Resources
- State Resources

# National Resources

| | HOUSING | | |
|---|---|---|---|
| Name | Website | Contact | Description |
| **Consumer Financial Protection Bureau** | consumerfinance.gov/housing/housing-insecurity/help-for-renters/get-help-paying-rent-and-bills | consumerfinance.gov/about-us/contact-us | Information on national and local resources for rent assistance and other housing costs |
| **Homeless Shelters Directory** | homelessshelterdirectory.org | | Unregulated nationwide directory of homeless shelters |
| **Low Income Home Energy Assistance Program- LIHEAP** | liheapch.acf.hhs.gov/search-tool | (866) 674-6327 energyhelp@ncat.org | Federal assistance for home energy costs (heating, repairs, etc.); details vary widely per state |
| **Shelter Listings** | shelterlistings.org | | Nationwide directory of homeless shelters, transitional housing, halfway houses, and more |
| **Transitional Housing** | transitionalhousing.org | (855) 860-3119 | Nationwide directory of low-cost or free temporary and transitional housing and substance use services |
| | ID | | |
| **US Social Security Office** | ssa.gov/locator | (800) 772-1213 | Request a replacement Social Security card, apply for retirement, disability, and Medicare benefits |
| **Vital Chek** | vitalchek.com | vitalchek-solutions.custhelp.com/app/ask | Government-authorized service for requesting certified copies of your birth certificate |
| | FOOD | | |
| **Feeding America** | feedingamerica.org/find-your-local-foodbank | | Nationwide directory of local food banks |
| **Food Pantries** | foodpantries.org | | Nationwide directory of local food banks, soup kitchens, and subsidized groceries |
| | HEALTHCARE | | |
| **AIDS Info Hotline** | HIVinfo.NIH.gov | (800) 448-0440 HIVinfo@NIH.gov 5600 Fishers Ln Rockville, MD 20857-9840 | Nationwide directory of local clinics and hotlines for confidential answers to questions about HIV/AIDS, treatments, and clinical trials |

Mapping Your Future, National Edition

#  National Resources

| Name | Website | Contact | Description |
|---|---|---|---|
| **EyeCare America** | aao.org/eyecare-america | (877) 887-6327<br>655 Beach St<br>San Francisco, CA<br>94109-1336 | Medical eye exams, often at no cost |
| **GoodRx** | goodrx.com | | Discount prescription service, most useful to uninsured people |
| **National Suicide Prevention Helpline** | 988lifeline.org/chat | 988 or<br>(800) 273-TALK (8255) | 24/7 suicide and mental health crisis lifeline, online chat available |
| **Ryan White HIV/AIDS program** | hab.hrsa.gov/get-care<br>Find state programs here: targethiv.org/community/find-services | (301) 443-1993 | Health Resources and Services Administration (HRSA) service helping low-income people to get HIV care, treatment, and support |
| **Transitions Clinic Network (TCN)** | transitionsclinic.org/locations | TCNinfo@ucsf.edu<br>1855 Folsom St,<br>San Francisco,<br>CA 94103 | Fourteen-state network of clinics for people who left prison with a chronic illness; offers training and employment for formerly incarcerated people interested in becoming community health workers |
| **US Healthcare Marketplace** | healthcare.gov | (800) 318-2596 | National website to sign up for health insurance, including Medicaid and Medicare services |
| **MENTAL HEALTH, WELLNESS, AND MINDFULNESS** | | | |
| **InsightTimer Phone App** | insighttimer.com<br><br>or by visiting the app store on your smartphone | | Meditation app with free access to thousands of guided meditations and mindfulness talks; includes content focusing on addiction and recovery<br><br>**For a primer on phone apps, please see "Smartphone Apps" in the Technology chapter, p. 86.** |
| **Palouse Mindfulness** | palousemindfulness.com | | Free online mindfulness-based stress reduction (MBSR) group **(See description of MBSR on p. 126)** |
| **Suicide and Crisis Lifeline** | 988lifeline.org | 988 | 24/7 suicide and mental health crisis lifeline; online chat available |
| **UCLA Mindful Phone App** | uclahealth.org/marc/ucla-mindful-app<br><br>or by visiting the app store on your smartphone | | Easy-to-use app with beginner meditations, wellness meditations for people suffering from challenging health conditions, scientific and how-to videos on mindfulness, and weekly podcasts on different meditation themes |

# National Resources

| SUBSTANCE USE SERVICES | | | |
|---|---|---|---|
| Name | Website | Contact | Description |
| Alcoholics Anonymous | aa.org | (212) 870-3400 | Nationwide network of online and in-person 12-step-program support groups |
| Narcotics Anonymous | na.org | (818) 773-9999 | Nationwide network of online and in-person 12-step-program support groups |
| Secular Organizations for Sobriety | sossobriety.org | (314) 353-3532 | Nationwide network of in-person and online non-religious peer groups to help people maintain sobriety |
| SAMSHA | findtreatment.gov | (800) 662-4357<br>(877) 726-4727<br>SAMHSAInfo@samhsa.hhs.gov | Information hub and national referral service for local treatment facilities, support groups, community-based organizations, and more |
| Women for Sobriety | womenforsobriety.org | (215) 536-8026 | Nationwide in-person and online peer-support program for women overcoming addiction |
| **REENTRY SERVICES** | | | |
| Fair Shake | fairshake.net | (608) 634-6363<br>P.O. Box 63<br>Westby, WI 54667 | Online reentry resources, including a basic toolkit, national reentry resources, and a nationwide directory of local reentry resources |
| **EMPLOYMENT & TRAINING** | | | |
| American Job Center | careeronestop.org | (877) 872-5627 | Online job-search tool |
| Best Accredited Colleges | study.com/resources/formerly-incarcerated-education-career-guide | info@bestaccreditedcolleges.org | A guide to help formerly incarcerated students and career-seekers find educational and employment opportunities |
| Jails to Jobs | jailstojobs.org | info@jailstojobs.org<br>3641 Mount Diablo Blvd, #1164<br>Lafayette, CA 94549 | Career-planning and job-search tools for people with criminal records |
| Jobs For Felons Hub | jobsforfelonshub.com | | Online job-search tool for people with felony records |
| Minnesota State's CareerWise | careerwise.minnstate.edu/exoffenders/workbook.html | (651) 361-7200 | Online job-planning workbook and job-search tool for people with a criminal conviction |

Mapping Your Future, National Edition

# National Resources

## LEGAL ASSISTANCE

| Name | Website | Contact | Description |
|---|---|---|---|
| **Executive Office for Immigration Review (EOIR)** | justice.gov/eoir/list-pro-bono-legal-service-providers | (703) 305-0289 | Department of Justice's national directory of pro bono immigration legal services |
| **Immigration Advocates Network** | immigrationadvocates.org/nonprofit/legaldirectory | | Nationwide directory of free or low-cost immigration legal services by state, county, or detention facility |
| **Legal Action Center** | clearinghouse.lac.org/public | (212) 243-1313<br>225 Varick St<br>4th Floor, New York, NY 10014 | Nationwide directory of legal and employment resources for people with criminal records |

## FAMILY & CHILDREN RESOURCES

| Name | Website | Contact | Description |
|---|---|---|---|
| **Domestic Violence Hotline** | thehotline.org | (800) 799-7233 text START to 88788; or live chat on website | Confidential, free 24-hour hotline for support, information, and local referrals |
| **National Diaper Network** | nationaldiaperbanknetwork.org/member-directory | (203) 821-7348<br>470 James St, #007 New Haven CT 06513 | Nationwide directory of local groups devoted to ending diaper need |

## BOOKS FOR CURRENTLY INCARCERATED PEOPLE

| Name | Website | Contact | Description |
|---|---|---|---|
| **LGBT Books to Prisoners** | lgbtbookstoprisoners.org | lgbtbookstoprisoners@gmail.com<br>1202 Williamson St, #1, Madison, WI 53703 | Mails free books to LGBTQ+ people in prison |
| **Prison Library Project** | prisonlibraryproject.org | (909) 626-3066<br>info@claremontforum.org<br>586 W 1st St Claremont, CA | Mails free books to people in prison with a focus on parenting from prison |

## VETERAN SERVICES

| Name | Website | Contact | Description |
|---|---|---|---|
| **US Department of Veterans Affairs** | va.gov/ogc/docs/legalservices.pdf | | State-by-state free legal clinics for veterans; services vary |
| **US Department of Veterans Affairs** | va.gov/homeless/reentry.asp | | Health care for re-entering veterans; aid in short-term case management, outreach, pre-release assessments, and medical referrals |
| **US Department of Veterans Affairs** | va.gov/ogc/apps/accreditation/accredvso.asp | | National search engine for veterans' services, offering a list of accredited veterans' service organizations |

**National Resources**

| Name | Website | Contact | Description |
|---|---|---|---|
| **Mindfulness Coach (Phone App)** | apps.apple.com/us/app/mindfulness-coach/id804284729<br><br>or by visiting the app store on your smartphone | | Free, private app created by the VA's National Center for PTSD but available to all; includes self-guided mindfulness training, resource library, exercises, and access to support and crisis resources<br><br>**(For a primer on phone apps, please see "Smartphone Apps" in the Technology chapter, p. 86)** |
| **U.S. Department of Veterans Affairs** | benefits.va.gov/PERSONA/veteran-incarcerated.asp | | Assistance for system-impacted veterans seeking access to their benefits; includes program descriptions |
| **Veteran Crisis Line** | 988lifeline.org | (800) 273-8255, text 838255 | 24/7 veterans' and service members' crisis line |
| **SOBER HOUSING** | | | |
| **Sober House Directory** | soberhousedirectory.com | soberhousedirectory.com/contact | National directory of sober houses and structured group homes (no halfway houses, treatment programs, or rehabilitation facilities) |
| **Substance Rehab Center** | substancerehabcenter.com/services/residential<br><br>substancerehabcenter.com/treatment-centers | (888) 844-3455 substancrehabcenter.com/contact-us | Nationwide directory of residential rehab facilities as well as outpatient services |

Mapping Your Future, National Edition

# State Resources

| State | Name | Website | Address | Phone/Email | Description |
|---|---|---|---|---|---|
| AK | Bristol Bay Native Association Reentry Program | bbna.com/bristol-bay-reentry-program | 1500 Kanakanak Rd Dillingham, AK 99576 | (907) 842-5257, contact@bbna.com | Reentry support, case management, referrals |
| AK | Ketchikan Reentry Coalition | ketchikanwellness.org | 602 Dock St #108, Ketchikan, AK 99901 | (907) 225-9355 info@ketchikanwellness.org | Resource guide, substance use support, reentry support, volunteer opportunities |
| AK | Mat-Su Reentry Program | valleycharities.org/mat-su-valley-reentry-program | | (907) 414-4077, barbara.mongar valleycharities.org | Community-based case management, reentry support |
| AK | New Life Development | newlifeak.org | 3916 E 9th Ave Anchorage, AK 99508 | (907) 646-2200 admin@newlifeak.org | Reentry support, substance use support |
| AK | No Limits, Inc. | nolimitincorg.wordpress.com | 253 Romans Way, Fairbanks, AK 99701 | (907) 451-9650, nolimits.exdir@yahoo.com | Reentry support, substance use support |
| AL | Aid to Inmate Mothers | inmatemoms.org | 660 Morgan Ave, Montgomery, AL 36104 | (334) 262-2245 | Family services |
| AL | The Foundry Ministries | foundryministries.com | Multiple Alabama locations | (205) 424-4673 | Substance use support |
| AL | The Lovelady Center | loveladycenter.org | Multiple Alabama locations | (205) 833-7410 | Employment opportunities, faith-based reentry support for women |
| AL | Renascence, Inc | halfway-home.net | 215 Clayton St, Montgomery, AL 36104 | (334) 832-1402, renascenceinc@outlook.com | Reentry support, transitional housing for men |
| AZ | Arizona Common Ground | arizonacommonground.org | PO Box 90990 Phoenix, AZ 85066 | (602) 914-9000, azcommonground@live.com | Reentry support |
| AZ | Hope's Crossing | hopescrossing.org | 1632 W Camelback Rd Phoenix, AZ 85015 | (602) 795-8098 | Family services, reentry support |

# State Resources

| State | Name | Website | Address | Phone/Email | Description |
|---|---|---|---|---|---|
| AZ | Old Pueblo Community Services | helptucson.org | 4501 E 5th St Tucson, AZ 85711 | (520) 546-0122, info@helptucson.org | Employment, housing, case management, therapy |
| AR | Arkansas Reentry Guide | arreentryguide.com/resources | C/O Foundation for the Mid South, 134 E Amite St, Jackson, MS 39201 | (601) 355-8167, arreentryguide@fndmidsouth.org | Directory of national, state, and local reentry resources |
| AR | Central Arkansas Reentry Coalition | facebook.com/arkansasreentry | 3805 W 12th St Little Rock, AR 72204 | (501) 444-2273, centralarkansasreentry@gmail.com | Reentry support, legal support, employment |
| AR | Little Rock Compassion Center | lrcompassioncenter.org | 3618 W Roosevelt Rd Little Rock, AR 72204 | (501) 296-9114 | Food, reentry support, substance use support, transitional housing |
| CA | Anti-Recidivism Coalition | antirecidivism.org | 1320 E 7th St #260, Los Angeles CA 90021 | (213) 955-5885, expungements@antirecidivism.org | Reentry support, employment, education and training, women's services, housing |
| CA | Bonafide | bonafidelife.org/index.php/our-organization | | | Reentry support, support groups |
| CA | California Reentry Program | ca-reentry.org | PO Box 483 San Quentin, CA 95964 | (415) 870-7020 info@ca-reentry.org | Reentry support, education and training, special-needs assistance |
| CA | Community Prisoner Mother Program | cdcr.ca.gov/adult-operations/fops/community-prisoner-mother-program | 1515 S St #415S Sacramento, CA 95811 | (909) 624-1233 Ext 2160 | Reentry support for mothers with children, family services |
| CA | CROP | croporganization.org | 2511 Adeline St Oakland CA 94607 | (341) 441-0159, info@croporg.org | Reentry support, education, technology support |
| CA | Homeboy Industries | homeboyindustries.org | 130 W Bruno St Los Angeles, CA 90012 | (323) 526-1254, info@homeboyindustries.org | Reentry support for former gang members |
| CA | Los Angeles Regional Reentry Partnership | lareentry.org | 724 N La Brea Blvd Inglewood, CA 90302 | info@lareentry.org | Reentry support, employment, housing, education |

Mapping Your Future, National Edition

# State Resources

| State | Name | Website | Address | Phone/Email | Description |
|---|---|---|---|---|---|
| CA | Mass Liberation | massliberation.net | 21519 Menlo Ave Torrance, CA 90502 | contact@massliberation.net | Education and empowerment, employment, reentry support, housing |
| CA | Root & Rebound | rootandrebound.org/resources/ca-roadmap | 1610 Harrison St, Ste E, East Oakland, CA 94612 | (510) 279-4662 info@rootandrebound.org | Comprehensive state reentry guide, employment, housing, legal services hotline |
| CA | Self Awareness and Recovery | selfawarenessrecovery.org | 4625 44th St #22 Sacramento, CA 95820 | (916) 490-6398, selfawarenessandrecovery@gmail.com | Mental health support, support groups, reentry support, education |
| CA | St. John's Community Center | sjch.org | 808 W 58th St Los Angeles, CA 90037 | (323) 541-1411 | Medical services, women's services |
| CA | The Green Life | thegreenlifeproject.org | 2150 Allston Way, #460 Berkeley, CA 94704 | angela4change@gmail.com | Education and training, education in prison |
| CA | Transitions Clinic | transitionsclinic.org/locations | Multiple locations | TCNinfo@ucsf.edu | Health clinic welcoming formerly incarcerated people, especially the chronically ill |
| CO | Focus Reentry | focusreentry.org/about-focus | 1905 15th St Boulder, CO 80306 | (720) 662-2577 info@focusreentry.org | Reentry support, housing, substance use support |
| CO | Remerg | remerg.com | PO Box 18463 Denver, CO 80218 | (303) 993-3551, carol@remerg.com | Reentry support, basic needs, family services |
| CO | Second Chance Center | scccolorado.org | 224 Potomac St, Aurora, CO 80011 | (303) 537-5838 info@SCCColorado.org | Education, employment, housing, mentoring |
| CO | The Reentry Initiative | reentryinitiative.org | 402 Kimbark St Longmont, CO 80501 | (720) 640-9513 info@reentryinitiative.org | Clothing assistance, reentry support, trauma-informed therapy |
| CT | Emerge | emergect.net | 830 Grand Ave New Haven, CT 06511 | (203) 562-0171, info@emergect.net | Employment assistance, reentry support |
| CT | Families in Crisis | familycenters.org/Families-in-Crisis | 60 Popieluszko Ct, Hartford, CT 06106 | info@familiesincrisis.org | Education, employment, healthcare |

# State Resources

| State | Name | Website | Address | Phone/Email | Description |
|---|---|---|---|---|---|
| CT | Transitions Clinic | transitionsclinic.org/locations | Multiple locations | TCNinfo@ucsf.edu | Health clinic welcoming formerly incarcerated people, especially the chronically ill |
| DE | Delaware Center for Justice | dcjustice.org | 100 W 10th St #905 Wilmington, DE 19801 | (302) 658-7174 center@dcjustice.org | Reentry support, advocacy, training and empowerment |
| DE | Partnership In Reentry Coalition of Delaware | pircod.org | | | Reentry support, family services, housing |
| DE | Project New Start | project-new-start.org | 4601 Concord Pike Wilmington, DE 19803 | (302) 478-2804 pturgon@project-new-start.org | Employment, education/training during reentry |
| DE | ReEntry Delaware | reentryde.org | 3434 Old Capitol Trl, Wilmington, DE 19808 | (302) 275-2799, reentryde3@gmail.com | Veterans' reentry support |
| DE | Sojourners' Place | sojournersplace.org/re-entry-services.html | 2901 NE Blvd, Wilmington, DE 19802 | (302) 764-4713 | Reentry support, residential program, case managed |
| DE | The Way Home Program | twhprogram.org | PO Box 1103, 7 S King St, Georgetown, DE 19947 | (302) 856-9870 director@twhprogram.org | Housing, education, therapy, employment, food, reentry and ongoing support |
| DE | Wilmington HOPE Commission | wilmhope.org | 38 Vandever Ave Wilmington, DE 19802 | (302) 407-3397 | Childcare, employment, healthcare, housing, reentry support, women's reentry program, therapy |
| FL | Covenant House Florida | covenanthousefl.org | 733 Breakers Ave, Fort Lauderdale, FL 33304 | (954) 561-5559 | Youth services including: housing, health services, substance use support, employment |
| FL | Operation New Hope | operationnewhope.org | Locations in Jacksonville, Orlando, St. Augustine, and on the Space Coast | (904) 354-4673 info@operationnewhope.org | Pre- and post-release education and job training, employment, housing, reentry support |

Mapping Your Future, National Edition

# State Resources

| State | Name | Website | Address | Phone/Email | Description |
|---|---|---|---|---|---|
| FL | Project 180 | project180@reentry.org | PO Box 25684 Sarasota, FL 34277-2684 | (941) 677-2281, ceo@project180reentry.org | Reentry support, residential program for men(exclusionary of some convictions) |
| GA | Liberty County Re-entry Coalition, Inc. | libertyreentry.org | 205 E Court St Hinesville, GA 31313 | (912) 877-5293 | Reentry support, housing, childcare, employment |
| GA | Our House | ourhousega.org | 173 Blvd NE Atlanta, GA 30312 (Second location in Decatur) | Atlanta: (404) 522-6056 Decatur: (404) 378-0938 hello@ourhousega.org | Focus on unhoused people: education, employment, family services, healthcare, transitional housing |
| GA | Reentry Partnership Housing (RPH) Program | cacj.georgia.gov/resources/reentry-partnership-housing-rph-program | | (678) 529-0307 christina.frazier@georgiacourts.gov | Housing, veterans, families, *excludes those with sex offense convictions or severe mental health problems* |
| GA | Transitional Housing for Offender Reentry (THOR) | sites.google.com/dcs.ga.gov/dcsreentryhousing/transitional-housing-for-offender-reentry-thor | | | Statewide directory of transitional housing offering substance use support and food assistance |
| HI | Going Home Hawai'i | goinghomehawaii.org | East: 80 Pauahi St #203 Hilo, HI 96720 West: 75-5708 Alahou St #2C Kailua-Kona, HI 96740 | East: (808) 491-2437 West: (808) 464-4003 | Family services, recovery-housing, reentry support, education, employment, mentoring |
| HI | WorkNet | worknetinc.org | 1130 N Nimitz Hwy #B-224 Honolulu, HI 96817 | (808) 521-7770, worknethawaii@gmail.com | Housing, reentry support, vocational training |
| ID | First Step 4 Life Recovery Community Center | facebook.com/firststep4life | 903 D St #201, Lewiston, ID 83501 | (208) 717-3881 info@firststep4life.org | Substance use support, recovery education, mental health support |
| ID | Recovery in Motion | recoveryinmotionrcc.org | 560 Shoup Ave W, Twin Falls, ID 83301 | (208) 712-2173, info@recoveryinmotionrcc.org | Free, peer-based mental health and substance use support |

# State Resources

| State | Name | Website | Address | Phone/Email | Description |
|---|---|---|---|---|---|
| ID | The Center for Hope | centerforhopeif.org | 530 E Anderson Idaho Falls, ID 83401 | (208) 538-1888 | Peer recovery, reentry support, substance use services |
| IA | Inside Out Reentry Community | insideoutreentry.com | 500 N Clinton St Iowa City, IA 52245 | (319) 338-7996 hello@insideoutreentry.com | Educational services, employment, housing, reentry support |
| IA | United Way of Central Iowa | unitedwaydm.org/opportunity | 1111 9th St #100, Des Moines, IA 50314 | (515) 246-6500, contactus@unitedwaydm.org | Government assistance, employment, housing, mental health support |
| IN | Life Outside Reentry Assistance | life-outside.org | | info@life-outside.org | Reentry support, employment, housing, mental health support, family services |
| KY | Community Action Kentucky | capky.org | 101 Burch Ct Frankfort, KY 40601 | (502) 875-5863 | Food security, transportation, housing, education, family services, and employment |
| KY | Kentucky Department of Public Advocacy, Capital Post Conviction Branch | dpa.ky.gov | 100 Fair Oaks Ln, Frankfort, KY 40601 | (502) 564-8006 | Legal services and referrals |
| KY | Life Coach Each One Teach One | lifecoacheachoneteachone.org | 1115 Garvin Pl Louisville, KY 40203 | (502) 438-9194, savvykashabazz@gmail.com | Employment, education, voting rights |
| LA | Community Service Center, Inc. | | 4000 Magazine St, New Orleans, LA 70115 | (504) 897-6277, cscnouw@aol.com | Reentry support, support groups, substance use support |
| LA | FIT Clinic at Healthcare for the Homeless | nhchc.org/health-care-for-the-homeless | Multiple locations | | Health clinic welcoming formerly incarcerated people, especially those who are chronically ill |
| LA | Goodwill Industries of Southeastern Louisiana, Inc. | goodwillno.org/programs/ex-offender-re-entry-program | 3400 Tulane Ave #1000, New Orleans, LA 70119 | (504) 456-2622 | Employment training and assistance |

Mapping Your Future, National Edition

# State Resources

| State | Name | Website | Address | Phone/Email | Description |
|---|---|---|---|---|---|
| ME | Maine Prisoner Advocacy Coalition | maineprisoneradvocacy.org | PO Box 446 Lisbon, ME 04250 | maineprisoneradvocacy@yahoo.com | Reentry resources, commitment to changes to Maine's prison system |
| ME | Maine Prisoner Re-Entry Network | re-entrymaine.org | PO Box 7157 Lewiston, ME 04240 | (207) 330-1446, info@re-entrymaine.org | Reentry support, housing, mental health support, statewide reentry resources network |
| ME | Reentry Sisters | reentrysisters.org | | (207) 852-7487 reentrysistersmaine@gmail.com | Women's services, reentry support, education, housing. |
| ME | Restorative Justice Project | rjpmidcoast.org | 39A Spring St Belfast, ME 04915 | (207) 338-2742 | Residential program based on restorative justice practices |
| MD | DHCDC ReEntry Program | druidheights.com/dhcdc-reentry-program | 2140 McCulloh St, Baltimore, MD 21217 | (410) 523-1350 | Reentry support, housing, anger management, conflict resolution, job training |
| MD | Maryland Reentry Resource Center | mdrrc.org | 77 West St #110 Annapolis, MD 21401 | (410) 429-0107, admin@mdrrc.org | Reentry support, employment, education |
| MD | Return Home Baltimore | sandbox.returnhome.org | | info@returnhome.org | Comprehensive reentry resources |
| MA | City of Boston Returning Citizens Department | boston.gov/departments/returning-citizens | 30 Dimock St 2nd Floor Roxbury, MA 02119 | (617) 541-3887 | Birth certificate retrieval, employment, healthcare, substance use support, voting |
| MA | Community Resources For Justice | crj.org | Multiple offices with varying services | (617) 482-2520, connect@crj.org | Reentry, education, mental health, health, employment, housing, substance use support |
| MA | Prisoners' Legal Services of Massachusetts | plsma.org | 10 Winthrop Sq Boston, MA 02110 | (617) 482-2773, lwalker@plsma.org | Legal services and referrals |
| MA | Volunteers of America Massachusetts | voamass.org | 441 Centre St Jamaica Plain, MA 02130 | (617) 522-8086, info@voamass.org | Reentry support, mental health support, substance use support, veteran services |

# State Resources

| State | Name | Website | Address | Phone/Email | Description |
|---|---|---|---|---|---|
| MI | A Brighter Way | abrighterway.org | 124 Pearl St #201, Ypsilanti, MI 48197 | (734) 896-3770, mentoring@abrighterway.org | Reentry support mentoring for Washington County |
| MN | AMICUS | voamnwi.org/amicus-reconnect | 3041 4th Ave Minnesota, MN 55048 | (612) 877-4250 | Reentry support, mentoring, support groups, housing |
| MN | Central Minnesota Reentry Project | cmnrp.org | PO Box 2391 St. Cloud, MN 56302 | (320) 656-9004 pat@cmnrp.org | Reentry support, anger management, family services |
| MN | Emerge | emerge-mn.org/reentry-services | 1834 Emerson Ave, North Minneapolis, MN 55411 | (612) 529-9267, info@emerge-mn.org | Reentry support, financial, housing, job training |
| MN | Hennepin Healthcare | hennepinhealthcare.org | Multiple locations | (612) 873-3000 | Health clinic for system-involved people, especially those who are chronically ill |
| MN | 180 Degrees | 180degrees.org/community-reentry.html | Multiple locations | (612) 813-5006, info@180degrees.org | Reentry support for men, housing, employment, mental health support, substance use support |
| MS | Mississippi Association for Returning Citizens (MARC) | marcreentry.org/ | St. Paul Catholic Church, 5971 Hwy 25 Flowood, MS 39232 | (601) 521-1331 dorothy@marcreentry.org | Reentry support, resource network, in-prison preparation |
| MS | Mississippi Center for Reentry | msreentry.org | 230-2 Goodman Rd E #202 Southaven, MS 38671 | (662) 701-6031, info@msreentry.org | Reentry support, education |
| MO | Humanitri | humanitri.org | PO Box 6512 St. Louis, MO 63125 | (314) 772-7720 | Transitional housing, case management for housing |
| MO | Missouri Reentry Program | theallianceofswmo.org/missouri-reentry-program | 1601 S Wall Ave Joplin, MO 64804 | (417) 782-9899, mdiggs@theallianceofswmo.org | Reentry support, employment, transportation, housing, mental health support, medical support |

Mapping Your Future, National Edition

# State Resources

| State | Name | Website | Address | Phone/Email | Description |
|---|---|---|---|---|---|
| MO | Power House Community Development | pwrhousecdc.org/fresh-start-missouri-reentry-program.html | 103 N Miami Ave, Marshall, MO 65340 | (660) 886-8860 info@pwrhousecdc.org | Reentry support, parenting programs, food, education, summer camps for dependents |
| MT | Community, Counseling, & Correctional Services | cccscorp.com/programs/gcrp | 675 S 16th Ave Bozeman, MT 59715 | (406) 494-0306, mhamblin@cccscorp.com | Reentry support, housing, substance use support |
| NE | Bridges to Hope | bridgestohopene.org | 3107 S 6th St #107, Lincoln, NE 68502 | (402) 420-5696 | Reentry support, basic necessities, housing, job training |
| NE | Community Justice Center | communityjusticecenter.org | 211 N 14th St #309, Lincoln, NE 68508 | (402) 277-8111, jim.jones@communityjusticecenter.org | Restorative justice support, employment, housing, skill development |
| NE | Reentry Alliance of Nebraska | re-entrynebraska.org | 1230 O St #240 Lincoln, NE 68508" | | Reentry support, job training, skill development, food, housing, substance use support, housing, clothing |
| NE | Released and Restored | releasedandrestored.org | PO Box 22962 Lincoln, NE 68542 | (402) 806-0565 info@releasedandrestored.org | Reentry support, skill development, employment, empowerment |
| NV | Foundation for an Independent Tomorrow | lasvegasfit.org | 1931 Stella Lake St, Las Vegas, NV 89106 | (702) 367-4348 | Case management, vocational training, job training, support services |
| NV | Foundation for Recovery | forrecovery.org | 4800 Alpine Pl #12, Las Vegas, NV 89107 | (702) 257-8199 info@forrecovery.org | Peer recovery, substance use support, mental health support |
| NV | Hope for Prisoners | hopeforprisoners.org | 333 N Rancho Las Vegas, NV | | Reentry support, financial training, leadership training, job readiness |
| NH | Dismas Home | dismashomenh.org | | (603) 782-3004 info@dismashomenh.org | Substance use rehabilitation for women |

# State Resources

| State | Name | Website | Address | Phone/Email | Description |
|---|---|---|---|---|---|
| NH | Head Rest | headrest.org | 141 Mascoma St Lebanon, NH 03766 | (603) 448-4872 | Crisis hotline for substance use, residential program, outpatient program, employee recovery |
| NJ | H.O.P.E For Ex-Offenders, Inc. | facebook.com/HOPEforExo | 259 Passaic St Hackensack, NJ 07601 | (201) 646-0234 | Reentry support, housing, education, employment |
| NJ | Reentry Coalition of New Jersey | reentrycoalitionofnj.org | 986 S Broad St Trenton, NJ 08611 | (609) 706-2684, info@reentrycoalitionofnj.org | Online resource directory |
| NJ | Reentry Corporation | njreentry.org | 591 Summit Ave, 6th Floor Jersey City, NJ 07306 | (551) 256-9717 | Nonprofit activism group, reentry resources |
| NJ | The Petey Greene Program | peteygreene.org | 22 Stockton St, Princeton, NJ 08540 | (877) 624-7186 pgp@peteygreene.org | Education, tutors |
| NM | A Peaceful Habitation | apeacefulhabitation.org | PO Box 53516 Albuquerque, NM 53516 | (505) 440-5937 | Reentry support for women, housing, mentoring, mental healthcare, skill development |
| NM | New Mexico Reentry Center | nmreentrycenter.org | 215 3rd St SW Albuquerque, NM 87102 | (505) 389-5458 natashag@nmwrc.org | Reentry support, case management, housing, employment |
| NY | Alliance of Families for Justice | afj-ny.org/contact | 8 W 126th St 3rd Floor, New York, NY 10027 | (347) 973-0580 info@afj-ny.org | Legal support, family support groups, resources |
| NY | Center for Employment Opportunities | ceoworks.org | 50 Broadway #1604, New York, NY 10004 | (212) 422-4430, info@ceoworks.org | Transitional employment, skill development, career support |
| NY | Columbia University Center for Justice | centerforjustice.columbia.edu | 1190 Amsterdam Ave, 219 Schermerhorn Hall and 1255 Amsterdam Ave, Room 828 New York, NY 10027 | centerforjustice@columbia.edu | Policy activism, college in prison, education after reentry, arts/media training for incarcerated youth, leadership development program |

#  State Resources

| State | Name | Website | Address | Phone/Email | Description |
|---|---|---|---|---|---|
| NY | Economic Opportunity Commission of Nassau County, Inc. | eoc-nassau.org/restore-to-life | 134 Jackson St Hempstead, NY 11550 | (516) 292-9710 | Reentry support, mentoring, housing, job, referrals |
| NY | Empire State University | sunyempire.edu/partnership-programs/community-partnerships/long-island-eoc | 2 Union Ave Saratoga Springs, NY 12866 | (800) 847-3000 | Flexible college program |
| NY | Exodus | etcny.org | 2268 3rd Ave New York, NY 10035 | (917) 492-0990, info@etcny.org | Reentry support, substance use support, employment, women's programs |
| NY | Fortune Society | fortunesociety.org | 29-76 Northern Blvd, Long Island City, NY 11101 | (212) 691-7554 info@fortunesociety.org | Reentry support, housing, employment, education, family services, substance use support, women's group |
| NY | Getting Out, Staying Out | gosonyc.org | 201A E 124th St New York, NY 10035 | (212) 831-5020, Info@gosonyc.org | Reentry support, education, employment, vocational training, case management |
| NY | Hudson Link for Higher Education in Prison | hudsonlink.org | PO Box 862, Ossining, NY 10562 | (914) 941-0794, info@hudsonlink.org | Policy activism, college-in-prison initiative |
| NY | Leadership Training Institute: Re-Entry Services | ltiny.org/programs-services/re-entry-services | 50 Clinton St #607 Hempstead, NY 11550 | (516) 483-3400, info@ltiny.org | Reentry support, family support, education, youth development, job training, economic mobility program |
| NY | Long Island Dismas House | svdpli.org/what-we-do/transitional-housing | 249 Broadway Bethpage, NY 11714 | (516) 822-3132, info@svdpli.org | Home visit analysis and services |
| NY | New York State: Reentry and College Access Organizations | justiceandopportunity.org/wp-content/uploads/2020/12/BackToSchoolGuide_ResourceGuide_final_pages.pdf | | | Higher education assistance, reentry task force listing, reentry coordinator listing |

# State Resources

| State | Name | Website | Address | Phone/Email | Description |
|---|---|---|---|---|---|
| NY | Osborne Association | osborneny.org | Bronx headquarters with multiple New York locations | (718) 707-2600, info@osborneny.org | Reentry support, job training, family services, housing, mental health services, substance use support |
| NY | The Institute for Justice and Opportunity | justiceandopportunity.org | 524 W 59th St #609B, New York, NY 10019 | JustOppInfo@jjay.cuny.edu | Education, employment, job training, advocacy |
| NY | Transitions Clinics | transitionsclinic.org/locations | Multiple locations | TCNinfo@ucsf.edu | Health clinic that welcomes formerly incarcerated people, especially those who are chronically ill |
| NY | Youth Represent | youthrepresent.org | 11 Park Pl #1512, New York, NY 10007 | (646) 759-8080 | Legal and social support for system-impacted youth under the age of 26 |
| NC | Center for Community Transitions | centerforcommunitytransitions.org | 5825 Old Concord Rd Charlotte, NC 28213 | (704) 494-0001 | Reentry support, family services, center for women |
| NC | Crossroads Reentry | crossroadsreentry.org | PO BOX 861 Huntersville, NC 28070 | (704) 499-1332, webinfo@crossroadsreentry.org | Reentry support, resource guides, substance use support, vocational training, housing |
| NC | Our Journey | ourjourney2gether.com | PO Box 2862 Rocky Mount, NC 27802 | (252) 220-9516, contact@ourjourney2gether.com | Reentry support, housing assistance |
| ND | F5 Project | f5project.org | 1122 1st Ave N Fargo, ND 58102 | (701) 210-2491, info@f5project.org | Reentry support, housing, employment, mental health support, substance use support |
| OH | Community Transition Program - Ohio Department of Mental Health and Addiction Services | mha.ohio.gov/community-partners/criminal-justice/re-entry-programs/community-transition-program-sitearea/community-transition-program | 30 E Broad St 36th floor Columbus, OH 43215-3430 | (614) 466-2596, Community.Linkage@mha.ohio.gov | Reentry support focused on preventive care and treatment for mental health and substance use |

Mapping Your Future, National Edition

# State Resources

| State | Name | Website | Address | Phone/Email | Description |
|---|---|---|---|---|---|
| OH | Lutheran Metropolitan Ministry | lutheranmetro.org | 4515 Superior Ave, Cleveland, OH 44113 | (216) 696-2715 mail@lutheranmetro.org | Housing, shelters for men, career services, youth shelter, youth center |
| OH | North Star Reentry Resource Center | northstarreentry.org | 1834 E 55th St Cleveland, OH 44103 | (216) 881-5440, NorthStarReentry@orianahouse.org | Education, mental health assistance, healthcare, employment, housing |
| OK | Hope for the Hopeless, Inc. | m.facebook.com/Hope-For-The-Hopeless-100151080048545 | 1301 W Sheridan Ave Oklahoma City, OK 73101 | hopeforthehopelessokc@hotmail.com | Ministry help to the homeless population in Oklahoma City, food and housing |
| OK | Inside Out Re-Entry Services | iors.org | 2224 E 56th Pl Tulsa, OK 74105 | (918) 949-4664 | Reentry support for women, faith-based programs, child reunification, housing, transportation, employment |
| OR | Helping Hands Reentry Outreach Center | helpinghandsreentry.org | PO Box 413 Seaside, OR 97138 | contact_us@helpinghandsreentry.org | Services for children and domestic violence survivors, case management, recovery groups, employment, housing |
| OR | Northwest Regional Reentry Center | nw-rrc.org | 6000 NE 80th Ave, Portland, OR 97218 | (503) 546-0470, info@nw-rrc.org | Reentry support, case management, employment, substance use support, mental health support, education, housing |
| OR | Prisoner Reentry Employment Program (PREP) | seworks.org/ex-offenders | 6401 SE Foster Rd, Portland, OR, 97206 | (503) 772-2300 | Employment, training services |
| OR | Sponsors, Inc. | sponsorsinc.org | 338 State Hwy 99 N Eugene, OR 97402 | (541) 485-8341, LJohnson@sponsorsinc.org | Case management, housing, mentoring, resource center, transportation, clothing, medical and mental health referrals, substance use support, therapy |

# State Resources

| State | Name | Website | Address | Phone/Email | Description |
|---|---|---|---|---|---|
| PA | Institute for Community Justice | icjphilly.org | 1207 Chestnut St, 2nd floor, Philadelphia, PA 19107 | (215) 525-0460 icj@fight.org | Free GED classes, case management, HIV resources, anger management, if eligible: a free cellular device and data |
| PA | Philadelphia RISE – Reintegration Services for Ex-Offenders | phila.gov/departments/office-of-reentry-partnerships | 1425 Arch St 1st floor Philadelphia, PA 19102 | (215) 683-3370, rise@phila.gov | Financial counseling, vocational training, education, mental health support |
| PA | Reimagine Reentry | letsreimaginereentry.org | 1901 Center Ave, #304 Pittsburgh, PA 15212 | info@letsreimaginereentry.org | Reentry support, housing, employment, family services |
| RI | Center for Primary Care, Lifespan | lifespan.org/locations/center-primary-care-rhode-island-hospital | | | Health clinic that welcomes formerly incarcerated people, especially those who are chronically ill |
| RI | Open Doors | opendoorsri.org | 485 Plainfield St Providence, RI 02909 | (401) 781-5805 admin@opendoorsri.org | Reentry support, resource center, employment, transitional housing |
| SC | Alston Wilkes Society | alstonwilkessociety.org | 3519 Medical Dr Columbia, SC 29203 | (803) 799-2490 | Housing, food, intense case management, veterans transitional housing, youth home services for males 11-21 who are referred |
| SC | Community Initiatives | communityinitiatives.us | 212 Overland Dr Greenwood, SC 29646 | (864) 223-7472, help@myci.us | After-school and summer program, medical clinic, senior services, job readiness training, benefit screening |
| SC | Root and Rebound | rootandrebound.org/locations/south-carolina | 222 Rutherford St, Greenville, SC 29609 | (864) 546-5089 | Reentry support, education, advocacy, reentry hot-line |
| SD | GEO Reentry Services | geogroup.com/Reentry-Services | Multiple | (561)-893-0101 | Reentry support, substance use support, anger management, housing |

Mapping Your Future, National Edition

# State Resources

| State | Name | Website | Address | Phone/Email | Description |
|---|---|---|---|---|---|
| SD | Lutheran Social Services of South Dakota | lsssd.org/what-we-do/re-entry-services/index.html | 705 E 41st St, #200, Sioux Falls, SD 57105 | (800) 568-2401, info@lsssd.org | Reentry support, counseling, financial resources, mentors, substance use support, employment |
| SD | South Dakota Dept. of Labor & Regulation Resources for Citizen Reentry | dlr.sd.gov/workforce_services/reentry/default.aspx | 123 W Missouri Ave, Pierre, SD 57501 | (605)-773-3101 | On-the-job training program, tuition assistance, job readiness development |
| TN | Chattanooga Endeavors | chattanoogaendeavors.org/about | PO Box 3351 Chattanooga, TN 37404 | (423) 266-1888, info@chattanoogaendeavors.org | Reentry support |
| TN | Dismas House | dismas.org/programs/re-entry-program | 2424 Charlotte Ave, Nashville, TN 37203 | (615) 297-4511 | Residential reentry program for men, legal support, life skill development, basic needs, health services |
| TN | Moving Forward, Tennessee Transitions | tennesseetransitions.org & Thei.org | 1006 Shelby Ave, Nashville, TN 37206 | 615-879-8857, info@thei.org | Comprehensive statewide reentry guide, reentry support, education |
| TN | Project Return | projectreturninc.org | 109 Lafayette St Nashville, TN 37210 | (615) 327-9654, pri@projectreturninc.org | Reentry support, job readiness development, case management, employment, housing |
| TN | State's Office of Reentry, Tennessee Department of Labor & Workforce Development | tn.gov/workforce/reentrytn.html | 220 French Landing Dr Nashville, TN 37243 | (844) 224-5818 | Reentry support, American job center links, legal services, voting registration, child and family services |
| TX | Goodwill Industries | goodwillhouston.org/jobs/job-career-services/mission-programs | 1140 W Loop N Houston, TX 77055 | (713) 692-6221 | Veterans employment and training services, reentry support: 18-24 years old |
| TX | Tarrant County Reentry Coalition | tcreentry.org | 3500 Noble Ave Fort Worth, TX 76111-4618 | (817) 632-6000, info@canetwork.org | Reentry resource guide coalition |

# State Resources

| State | Name | Website | Address | Phone/Email | Description |
|---|---|---|---|---|---|
| TX | Texas County Resources Map | countyresources.texascjc.org | | | Map of reentry resources throughout the state |
| TX | Texas Offenders Reentry Initiative | medc-tori.org | PO Box 4386 Dallas, TX 75208; 1270 Woodhaven Blvd #5245, Fort Worth, TX 76112 | (214) 941-1325 ext. 101, tori@tdjakes.org | Reentry support, healthcare, housing, education, employment, spirituality support, family intervention |
| TX | University of North Texas Department of Criminal Justice | hps.unt.edu/cjus/welcome-criminal-justice | | | Education, comprehensive reentry guide |
| TX | Unlocking Doors (Dallas) | unlockingdoors.org | 12225 Greenville Ave #850, Dallas, TX 75243 | (214) 296-9258, info@unlockingdoors.org | Reentry support with an intake form and a fee of $10, family support services, referrals |
| UT | Active Re-entry | arecil.org | 10 S Fairgrounds Rd Price, UT 84501 | (435) 637-4950, active@arecil.org | Reentry support, referrals to resources, life skill development, living programs for disability, counseling |
| UT | Golden Spike Outreach | facebook.com/people/Golden-Spike-Outreach/100067808450638 | 869 S 170 East Provo, UT 84601 | (801) 592-6001, richard@goldenspikeoutreach.com | Facebook charity group, reentry support, housing, substance use support |
| VT | Burlington Community Justice Center | burlingtoncjc.org/community-re-entry-cosa | 200 Church St Burlington, VT 05401 | (802) 865-7155 | Reentry support, employment, peer groups |
| VT | Reentry Essentials Inc. | reentryessentials.org | 2609 E 14 St, #1018 Brooklyn, NY 11235-3915 | info@reentryessentials.org | Reentry resource PDF |
| VT | Vermonters for Criminal Justice Reform | vcjr.org | 109 Bank St Burlington, VT 05401 | (802) 540-0440, tom@vcjr.org | Reentry and recovery center, focus on substance use support |
| VA | Offender Aid and Restoration of Arlington County | oaronline.org | 1400 N Uhle St Arlington, VA 22201 | (703) 228-7030 | Psychotherapy, vocational training, education, employment, housing |

Mapping Your Future, National Edition

# State Resources

| State | Name | Website | Address | Phone/Email | Description |
|---|---|---|---|---|---|
| VA | Opportunities, Alternatives & Resources of Fairfax County | oarfairfax.org | 10700 Page Ave #200, Fairfax, VA 22030 | (703) 246-3033, info@oarnova.org | Reentry support, violence intervention, family services, employment |
| VA | Virginia CARES | vacares.org | 108 Henry St NW, Third floor, Roanoke, VA 24016 | (540) 342-9344 jcarter@vacares.org | Reentry support and resource guide, housing, employment, family counseling, referrals, job readiness |
| WA | Arms Around You | armsaroundyou.org | 506 2nd Ave #1400, Seattle, WA 98030 | (206) 629-6405 armsaroundyou.org@gmail.com | Reentry support, vocational training, employment, peer counseling, life skill development, housing |
| WA | Country Doctor Community Health Center | cdchc.org | Multiple Seattle locations | | Health clinic that welcomes formerly incarcerated people |
| WA | Freedom Project | freedomprojectwa.org | 227 ½ Wells Ave S, Renton, WA 98057 | (206) 325-5678, connect@freedomprojectwa.org | Reentry support, counseling, resource referrals |
| WA | Interaction Transition | interactiontransition.org | 5300 4th Ave S, Seattle, WA 98108 | (206) 228-4639, it@interactiontransition.org | Reentry support, employment, prison outreach, peer mentoring |
| WA | Native American Reentry Services | nativereentry.org | 724 Yakima Ave 2nd floor, Tacoma, WA 98405 | (253) 212-9227 | Traditional and ceremonial reentry program, sweat lodge, case management, housing, education, employment, technology support |
| WA | New Connections | nctacoma.org | 613 S 15th St, Tacoma, WA 98405 | (253) 617-1405 | Women's reentry support, shelters, resource guide, community support |
| WA | Prison Scholar Fund | prisonscholars.org | 1752 NW Market St, Seattle, WA 98107 | (206) 734-5425 | Distance educational services, mentoring, educational advising |
| WA | Restored and Revived | restoredandrevived.com | 9317 NE Hwy 99 Ste J, Vancouver, WA 98665 | (360) 980-6428 info@restoredandrevived.com | Case management, family reunification, job readiness |

# State Resources

| State | Name | Website | Address | Phone/Email | Description |
|---|---|---|---|---|---|
| WA | Rotary Gig Harbor Women's Prison Program | rotarywomensprison.com | PO Box 342 Gig Harbor, WA 98335 | (253) 851-5575, rotarywomensprison@gmail.com | Reentry support for women: Employment training, educational scholarships, online mentoring |
| WA | Seattle Clemency | seattleclemencyproject.org | 20415 72nd Ave S #1-415, Kent, WA 98032 | (206) 682-1114, info@seattleclemencyproject.org | Pre-release program, reentry support, mentoring group, financial literacy class, career development |
| WA | The Journey Project | thejourneyproject.info | 13504 Tukwila International Blvd, Tukwila, WA 98168 | (206) 856-3125, transition@thejourneyproject.info | Reentry support, case management, housing, vocational training, job readiness skill development |
| WA | The Star Project | thestarproject.us | 321 Wellington Ave, PO Box 159 Walla Walla, WA 99362 | (509) 525-3612, info@thestarproject.us | Housing, employment, family reunification, substance use support |
| WA | House of Mercy: The Washington State Strong Foundation Reentry Guide | ReentryWa.com | | (206) 651-7840, reentryguide@hom.church | Reentry support, online reentry guide |
| WA | Weld Seattle | weldseattle.org | 1426 S Jackson Seattle, WA 98144 | (206) 567-9030, jay@weldseattle.org | Membership-based transitional housing recovery program, employment, resource referrals |
| WV | State Agency Directory | pds.wv.gov/community-resources/Pages/client-resources.aspx | One Players Club Dr, #301, Charleston, VW 25311 | (304) 558-3905 | Statewide services directory |
| WV | The REACH Initiative | wvreentry.org | 2207 Washington St E Charleston, WV 25311 | (855) 987-3224, reachjusticewv@gmail.com | Reentry support, referrals, backpack program providing necessities for the first week |
| WV | West Virginia Reentry Council | wvreentry.org/councils | | (304) 315-4796 bsharp@wvcc.org | Reentry support |

# State Resources

| State | Name | Website | Address | Phone/Email | Description |
|---|---|---|---|---|---|
| WV | Workforce West Virginia | workforcewv.org | Multiple locations | (800) 252-5627 | State-run employment assistance |
| WI | Benedict Center | benedictcenter.org | 1849 N Dr. Martin Luther King Dr #101, Milwaukee, WI 53212 | (414) 347-1774 | Reentry support for women, mental health support, substance use support, support for women involved in sex work |
| WI | Clean Slate Milwaukee | cleanslatemke.org | | (855) 947-2529, cleanslate.wi@gmail.com | Reentry support focusing on expungement services, resource referrals |
| WI | Journey Home | justdane.org/journey-home | 2115 S Park St Madison, WI 53713 | (608) 256-0906 info@justdane.org | Reentry support, case management, employment, family services |
| WI | LIFT Wisconsin | liftwisconsin.org | Dane County Job Center 1819 Aberg Ave, Madison, WI 53704 | (608) 242-7431 | Free legal support, resource database |
| WI | Project RETURN | projectreturnmilwaukee.org | 2821 Vel R Phillips Ave #223, Milwaukee, WI 53212 | (414) 374-8029 | Reentry support, housing, employment, substance use counseling |
| WY | Laramie Interfaith | laramieinterfaith.org | 712 Canby St Laramie, WY 82070 | (307) 742-4240 info@laramieinterfaith.org | Food assistance program, rental and utilities assistance |
| WY | Second Chance Ministries | secondchancegillette.org | 706 Longmont St Gillette, WY 82716 | (307) 682-3148 | Ministry-based, resources, transportation, document recovery, counseling, mentors |
| WY | Volunteers of America Northern Rockies - Booth Hall | voanr.org/services/adult-re-entry | 1876 S Sheridan Ave Sheridan, WY 82801 | (307) 682-8505 | Residential reentry program, individual reintegration plans, financial assistance, and employment. Veterans services, youth services, mental health support, substance use support, housing |

# Part 5: Forms

- Social Security Card Request Form
- Sample Resumes
- Veterans Beneficiary Apportionment Form

☆ *The Veterans Beneficiary form may be out of date when you read this. Download current apportionment forms here: www.va.gov/find-forms/about-form-21-0788*

Form **SS-5** (10-2021) UF
Use (11-2019) UF Until Stock Is Exhausted
SOCIAL SECURITY ADMINISTRATION

OMB No. 0960-0066

## Application for a Social Security Card

| 1 | **NAME** TO BE SHOWN ON CARD | First | Full Middle Name | Last |
|---|---|---|---|---|
| | FULL NAME AT BIRTH IF OTHER THAN ABOVE | First | Full Middle Name | Last |
| | OTHER NAMES USED | | | |

**2** Social Security number previously assigned to the person listed in item 1 ☐☐☐ – ☐☐ – ☐☐☐☐

**3** **PLACE OF BIRTH** (Do Not Abbreviate) City — State or Foreign Country — Office Use Only FCI

**4** **DATE OF BIRTH** MM/DD/YYYY

**5** **CITIZENSHIP** (Check One)
☐ U.S. Citizen ☐ Legal Alien Allowed To Work ☐ Legal Alien **Not** Allowed To Work (See Instructions On Page 3) ☐ Other (See Instructions On Page 3)

**6** **ETHNICITY** Are You Hispanic or Latino? (Your Response is Voluntary) ☐ Yes ☐ No

**7** **RACE** Select One or More (Your Response is Voluntary)
☐ Native Hawaiian ☐ American Indian ☐ Other Pacific Islander
☐ Alaska Native ☐ Black/African American ☐ White
☐ Asian

**8** **SEX** ☐ Male ☐ Female

**9**
A. PARENT/ MOTHER'S NAME AT HER BIRTH — First, Full Middle Name, Last
B. PARENT/ MOTHER'S SOCIAL SECURITY NUMBER (See instructions for 9B on Page 3) ☐☐☐ – ☐☐ – ☐☐☐☐ ☐ Unknown

**10**
A. PARENT/ FATHER'S NAME — First, Full Middle Name, Last
B. PARENT/ FATHER'S SOCIAL SECURITY NUMBER (See instructions for 10B on Page 3) ☐☐☐ – ☐☐ – ☐☐☐☐ ☐ Unknown

**11** Has the person listed in item 1 or anyone acting on his/her behalf ever filed for or received a Social Security number card before?
☐ Yes (If "yes" answer questions 12-13) ☐ No ☐ Don't Know (If "don't know," skip to question 14.)

**12** Name shown on the most recent Social Security card issued for the person listed in item 1 — First, Full Middle Name, Last

**13** Enter any different date of birth if used on an earlier application for a card — MM/DD/YYYY

**14** **TODAY'S DATE** MM/DD/YYYY

**15** **DAYTIME PHONE NUMBER** Area Code — Number

**16** **MAILING ADDRESS** (Do Not Abbreviate) — Street Address, Apt. No., PO Box, Rural Route No. — City — State/Foreign Country — ZIP Code

I declare under penalty of perjury that I have examined all the information on this form, and on any accompanying statements or forms, and it is true and correct to the best of my knowledge.

**17** YOUR SIGNATURE

**18** YOUR RELATIONSHIP TO THE PERSON IN ITEM 1 IS:
☐ Self ☐ Natural Or Adoptive Parent ☐ Legal Guardian ☐ Other Specify

---

DO NOT WRITE BELOW THIS LINE (FOR SSA USE ONLY)

| NPN | | | DOC | NTI | CAN | | ITV |
|---|---|---|---|---|---|---|---|
| PBC | EVI | EVA | EVC | PRA | NWR | DNR | UNIT |

EVIDENCE SUBMITTED

SIGNATURE AND TITLE OF EMPLOYEE(S) REVIEWING EVIDENCE AND/OR CONDUCTING INTERVIEW

DATE

DCL — DATE

# JOHN ALBERT **JOHNSON**

500 Main St, Anytown, IL 60606 · (555) 555-0000
JohnJohnson@email.com

## EXPERIENCE

**2015 TO PRESENT**
**ENGLISH TEACHER**
ADULT LEARNING CENTER, CHICAGO, IL
Coordinate community outreach efforts and administer institutional examinations.

**MARCH 2013-DECEMBER 2014**
**TEMP WORKER**
FRIENDLY TEMP AGENCY, CHICAGO, IL
Various assignments involving administrative and clerical roles

**AUGUST 2010-JANUARY 2013**
**TEACHER, PEER TUTOR**
ILLINOIS CENTRAL COMMUNITY COLLEGE, DECATUR, IL
Developed lesson plans, tutored beginning and advanced students.

## EDUCATION

**JUNE 2011-2012**
**ILLINOIS CENTRAL COMMUNITY COLLEGE**
ASSOCIATE'S DEGREE IN GENERAL STUDIES

- Education coursework: Advanced mathematics, Linguistics for language teachers, Political and historical perspectives in Education, Sociology of Education, Philosophy of Education

CERTIFICATE, PEER COUNSELING

**2009**
**NORTHERN ILLINOIS COMMUNITY COLLEGE**
CERTIFICATE IN HORTICULTURE STUDIES

## REFERENCES

Sharon Mendez, Coordinator
Adult Learning Center
1010 Center Street
Our Town, IL 60000
sharonmendez@email.com
555.555.5555

William Smith, Director
Friendly Temp Agency
40 North Ave.
Our Town, IL 66666
williamsmith@email.com
555.555.5555

# John Smith

## Contact
123 W. Main St. #5
Peoria, IL 60000
John.smith22@gmail.com
300-600-1234

## Education

University of Illinois Urbana-Champaign
July 2012-March 2014
*Upper-division courses in literature, communication, and theater.*
GPA: 4.0

Danville Area Community College
*Earned over 60 credits in toward an Associate's degree*
GPA: 4.0

## Key Skills
Kitchen equipment and sanitation
Special diet preparation
Conflict resolution
Creative and academic writing
Mentoring
Inventory, order, and stocking
Leadership in theater troupe

## Objective
My goal is to become associated with a company where I can utilize my skills and gain further experience while enhancing the company's productivity and reputation

## Experience

Resource Room Worker • Education Justice Project
July 2012-March 2014
*Assisted students with library needs, assisted tutors with tech support, conducted library circulation work, kept rooms cleaned and well organized*

Teaching Assistant • Adult Basic Education, State of Illinois
Dec 2015-Dec 2016
*Tutored students in basic literacy and numeracy for the Test of Adult Basic Education, graded student work, and maintained student records.*

Special Diet Cook • State of Illinois
1997-2015
*Operated commercial ovens, fryers, steam pots, and other equipment, prepared special diets, served meals in high capacity cafeteria*

## Publications and Awards

"Rhetorical Listening" (essay) Intertext, 2014
"Practicing Openness in Prison Education: A Collaborative Inquiry Into Empathic Pedagogy and the Politics of Compassion in Writing Center Practice." College Composition and Communication Conference, 2014
Prison Writing (essay). College Composition and Communication Conference, 2014
Martha Webber Creative Nonfiction Award, 2013.
Education Justice Project Creative Writing Award in Poetry, 2012

## References

Maggie Jones, Associate Professor of Sociology
University of IL-Springfield
j.ones@gmail.com 600-300-4000

Fred Thomas, General Manager
Smith Foundation
1323 Main St., Peoria, IL 60000
f.thomas@email.com 300-400-5000

# Alexis Williams

123 Main St., Chicago, IL 60000 | 312-555-5555 | petersmith@gmail.com

## Experience

University of Illinois
**ESL INSTRUCTOR**  2011-2014
- Served as a volunteer ESL instructor in Danville, IL to provide a much needed ESL class in the community
- Developed and taught lesson plans and activities in a multi-instructor class.
- Shared instructor responsibilities with 7 other instructors in a class of 10-12 students twice a week for a total of six hours with beginner-intermediate students
- Taught reading and writing for communicating effectively in personal and workplace settings.
- Provided corrective language feedback on oral and written production.

University of Illinois
**CHICAGO/COMMUNITY ANTI-VIOLENCE EDUCATION (CAVE)**  2011-2014
- Helped design and implement a peer driven anti-violence program that empowers incarcerated men through mentoring, education and character building to return to their communities as peace makers.

Danville Correctional Center (Clinical Services)
**GUEST SPEAKER/SUBSTANCE ABUSE INSTRUCTOR**  2011-2014
- Designed and presented lessons relating to substance abuse prevention to students at Danville Correctional Center

**PEACEFUL SOLUTIONS EDUCATOR**  2010-2011
- Designed and presented lessons focused on peaceful solutions for conflict resolution

## Education

**GOVERNOR'S STATE UNIVERSITY**  JUNE 2016
- Bachelor's Degree in Interdisciplinary Studies

**CARL SANDBERG COLLEGE, GALESBURG IL**  2000-2001
- Associate's Degree in General Education
- Business Management Certificate
- GPA: 3.38

**CERTIFIED ASSOCIATE'S ADDICTION PROFESSIONAL CERTIFICATION**  2012

## Skills

- Fluent in Spanish and English
- Microsoft Word, Access, Excel, PowerPoint

OMB Approved No. 2900-0666
Respondent Burden: 30 minutes
Expiration Date: 7/31/2024

# Department of Veterans Affairs

## INFORMATION REGARDING APPORTIONMENT OF BENEFICIARY'S AWARD

**VA DATE STAMP**
(DO NOT WRITE IN THIS SPACE)

**INSTRUCTIONS:** Before completing this form, read the Privacy Act and Respondent Burden on page 2. All or part of a veteran's disability award may be apportioned (paid) to the veteran's spouse, child, or dependent parent. A surviving spouse's award may also be apportioned for the veteran's child or children. If you are certifying that you are married for the purpose of VA benefits, your marriage must be recognized by the place where you and/or your spouse resided at the time of marriage, or where you and/or your spouse resided when you filed your claim (or a later date when you became eligible for benefits) (38 U.S.C. § 103(c)). For additional space, or to describe any financial hardship (not otherwise reflected on this form) you are experiencing or will experience based on the outcome of this claim, use Part III - Remarks. For more information, contact us at https://iris.custhelp.va.gov, or call us toll-free at 1-800-827-1000. If you use a Telecommunications Device for the Deaf (TDD), the Federal relay number is 711. VA forms are available at www.va.gov/vaforms. After completing the form, mail to: **Department of Veterans Affairs, Evidence Intake Center, P.O. Box 4444, Janesville, WI 53547-4444.**

| 1. VETERAN'S NAME (First, Middle Initial, Last) | 2. VA FILE NUMBER (If known) C/CSS- |
|---|---|
| 3A. PERSON COMPLETING THIS FORM (First, Middle Initial, Last) (If other than veteran) | 3B. MAILING ADDRESS (Number and street or rural route, city or P.O., State and ZIP Code) |

| 3C. TELEPHONE NUMBER (Include Area Code) | | 3D. E-MAIL ADDRESS (If applicable) |
|---|---|---|
| Daytime | Evening | |

| 4A. WHO ARE YOU REQUESTING AN APPORTIONMENT FOR? (List first, middle initial, and last names) | 4B. WHAT IS HIS/HER RELATIONSHIP TO THE VETERAN? |
|---|---|

| 5A. HOW MUCH IS THE VETERAN OR VETERAN'S SURVIVING SPOUSE CONTRIBUTING TO THE PERSON(S) FOR WHOM AN APPORTIONMENT IS BEING CLAIMED? $ | 5B. HOW OFTEN ARE THE CONTRIBUTIONS MADE? |
|---|---|

| 6. IF THE SPOUSE IS CLAIMING AN APPORTIONMENT, IS HE/SHE LIVING WITH ANOTHER PERSON AND HOLDING HIMSELF/HERSELF OUT OPENLY TO THE PUBLIC AS THE SPOUSE OF THE OTHER PERSON? ☐ YES ☐ NO (If "Yes," provide an explanation in Part III - Remarks): | 7. HAS THE VETERAN'S CHILD(REN) BEEN LEGALLY ADOPTED BY ANOTHER PERSON? ☐ YES ☐ NO |
|---|---|

### PART I - INCOME AND NET WORTH

Report all income and net worth. Report the gross amounts before you take out deductions for taxes, insurance, etc. If you do not receive income or net worth from a particular source, write "0" or "none" in the space provided. **Do not leave the space blank.** *Note:* If you are the veteran or surviving spouse, report only your income and net worth. If you are the claimant or are filing on behalf of the claimant(s), report all income and net worth for all persons for whom an apportionment is being claimed. If you are claiming an apportionment as the custodian of the veteran's child or children, report your income and net worth and the income and net worth of the child(ren).

#### MONTHLY INCOME

| SOURCE | VETERAN OR SURVIVING SPOUSE | CUSTODIAN | PERSON APPORTIONMENT IS CLAIMED FOR | PERSON APPORTIONMENT IS CLAIMED FOR |
|---|---|---|---|---|
| 1A. GROSS WAGES FROM ALL EMPLOYMENT | $ | $ | $ | $ |
| 1B. SOCIAL SECURITY | | | | |
| 1C. RETIREMENT OR ANNUITIES | | | | |
| 1D. SUPPLEMENTAL SECURITY INCOME (SSI) / PUBLIC ASSISTANCE | | | | |
| 1E. OTHER INCOME (Show source) | | | | |
| 1F. OTHER INCOME (Show source) | | | | |

#### NET WORTH

| SOURCE | VETERAN OR SURVIVING SPOUSE | CUSTODIAN | PERSON APPORTIONMENT IS CLAIMED FOR | PERSON APPORTIONMENT IS CLAIMED FOR |
|---|---|---|---|---|
| 2A. CASH/NON-INTEREST-BEARING BANK ACCOUNTS | $ | $ | $ | $ |
| 2B. INTEREST-BEARING BANK ACCOUNTS | | | | |
| 2C. IRAS, KEOGH PLANS, ETC. | | | | |
| 2D. STOCKS, BONDS, MUTUAL FUNDS, ETC. | | | | |
| 2E. REAL PROPERTY (Not your home) | | | | |
| 2F. ALL OTHER PROPERTY AND ASSETS | | | | |

VA FORM JUL 2021 **21-0788**  SUPERSEDES VA FORM 21-0788, MAR 2018.

## PART II - MONTHLY LIVING EXPENSES

Show your monthly living expenses, including any monthly installment payments. If you do not have expenses from a particular source, write "0" or "none" in the space provided. Do not leave the space blank.

Note: If you are the veteran or surviving spouse, report only your expenses. If you are the claimant or are filing on behalf of the claimant(s), report expenses for all persons for whom an apportionment is being claimed. If you are claiming an apportionment as the custodian of the veteran's child or children, report your expenses and the expenses of the child(ren).

| SOURCE | VETERAN OR SURVIVING SPOUSE | CUSTODIAN | PERSON APPORTIONMENT IS CLAIMED FOR | PERSON APPORTIONMENT IS CLAIMED FOR |
|---|---|---|---|---|
| 1A. RENT OR HOUSE PAYMENT | $ | $ | $ | $ |
| 1B. FOOD | | | | |
| 1C. UTILITIES *(Water, gas, electricity)* | | | | |
| 1D. TELEPHONE | | | | |
| 1E. CLOTHING | | | | |
| 1F. MEDICAL EXPENSES | | | | |
| 1G. SCHOOL EXPENSES | | | | |
| 1H. OTHER EXPENSES *(Show source)* | | | | |
| 1I. OTHER EXPENSES *(Show source)* | | | | |

## PART III - REMARKS

8. REMARKS

## PART IV - CERTIFICATION AND SIGNATURE

**I CERTIFY THAT** the foregoing statements are true and correct to the best of my knowledge and belief.

| 9. SIGNATURE OF VETERAN OR CLAIMANT (Required)  | 10. DATE SIGNED *(MM/DD/YYYY)* |
|---|---|

**PENALTY** - The law provides severe penalties which include fine or imprisonment or both, for the willful submission of any statement or evidence of a material fact, knowing it is false, or fraudulent acceptance of any payment to which you are not entitled.

**PRIVACY ACT INFORMATION** - The VA will not disclose information collected on this form to any source other than what has been authorized under the Privacy Act of 1974 or Title 38, Code of Federal Regulations 1.576 for routine uses (i.e., civil or criminal law enforcement, congressional communications, epidemiological or research studies, the collection of money owed to the United States, litigation in which the United States is a party or has an interest, the administration of VA programs and delivery of VA benefits, verification of identity and status, and personnel administration) as identified in the VA system of records, 58VA 21/22/28, Compensation, Pension, Education and Veteran Readiness and Employment Records - VA, published in the Federal Register. Your obligation to respond is required to obtain or retain benefits. The requested information is considered relevant and necessary to determine maximum benefits under the law. The responses you submit are considered confidential (38 U.S.C. 5701). Information submitted is subject to verification through computer matching programs with other agencies.

**RESPONDENT BURDEN** - We need this information to determine whether an apportionment of VA disability or death benefits may be made (38 U.S.C. 5307). Title 38, United States Code, allows us to ask for this information. We estimate that you will need an average of 30 minutes to review the instructions, find the information, and complete this form. VA cannot conduct or sponsor a collection of information unless a valid OMB control number is displayed. You are not required to respond to a collection of information if this number is not displayed. Valid OMB control numbers can be located on the OMB Internet Page at www.reginfo.gov/public/do/PRAMain. If desired, you can call 1-800-827-1000 to get information on where to send comments or suggestions about this form.